Classic
Rock Climbs

Garden
of the
Gods
Colorado

Bob D'Antonio

CHOCKSTONE®

FALCONGUIDES ®

GUILFORD, CONNECTICUT
HELENA, MONTANA

AN IMPRINT OF THE GLOBE PEQUOT PRESS

FALCONGUIDES®

Topo photos by Bob D'Antonio and Stewart M. Green

Library of Congress Cataloging-in-Publication Data is available on file.

ISBN 978-1-56044-678-1

Printed in the United States of America
10 9 8 7 6 5 4 3

WARNING:
CLIMBING IS A SPORT WHERE YOU MAY BE SERIOUSLY INJURED OR DIE. READ THIS BEFORE YOU USE THIS BOOK.

This guidebook is a compilation of unverified information gathered from many different climbers. The author cannot assure the accuracy of any of the information in this book, including the topos and route descriptions, the difficulty ratings, and the protection ratings. These may be incorrect or misleading and it is impossible for any one author to climb all the routes to confirm the information about each route. Also, ratings of climbing difficulty and danger are always subjective and depend on the physical characteristics (for example, height), experience, technical ability, confidence and physical fitness of the climber who supplied the rating. Additionally, climbers who achieve first ascents sometimes underrate the difficulty or danger of the climbing route out of fear of being ridiculed if a climb is later down-rated by subsequent ascents. Therefore, be warned that you must exercise your own judgment on where a climbing route goes, its difficulty, and your ability to safely protect yourself from the risks of rock climbing. Examples of some of these risks are: falling due to technical difficulty or due to natural hazards such as holds breaking, falling rock, climbing equipment dropped by other climbers, hazards of weather and lightning, your own equipment failure, and failure or absence of fixed protection.

You should not depend on any information gleaned from this book for your personal safety; your safety depends on your own good judgment, based on experience and a realistic assessment of your climbing ability. If you have any doubt as to your ability to safely climb a route described in this book, do not attempt it.

The following are some ways to make your use of this book safer:

1. Consultation: You should consult with other climbers about the difficulty and danger of a particular climb prior to attempting it. Most local climbers are glad to give advice on routes in their area and we suggest that you contact locals to confirm ratings and safety of particular routes and to obtain first-hand information about a route chosen from this book.

2. Instruction: Most climbing areas have local climbing instructors and guides available. We recommend that you engage an instructor or guide to learn safety techniques and to become familiar with the routes and hazards of the areas described in this book. Even after you are proficient in climbing safely, occasional use of a guide is a safe way to raise your climbing standard and learn advanced techniques.

3. Fixed Protection: Many of the routes in this book use bolts and pitons which are permanently placed in the rock. Because of variances in the manner of placement, weathering, metal fatigue, the quality of the metal used, and many other factors, these fixed protection pieces should always be considered suspect and should always be backed up by equipment that you place yourself. Never depend for your safety on a single piece of fixed protection because you never can tell whether it will hold weight, and in some cases, fixed protection may have been removed or is now absent.

Be aware of the following specific potential hazards which could arise in using this book:

1. Misdescriptions of Routes: If you climb a route and you have a doubt as to where the route may go, you should not go on unless you are sure that you can go that way safely. Route descriptions and topos in this book may be inaccurate or misleading.

2. Incorrect Difficulty Rating: A route may, in fact, be more difficult than the rating indicates. Do not be lulled into a false sense of security by the difficulty rating.

3. Incorrect Protection Rating: If you climb a route and you are unable to arrange adequate protection from the risk of falling through the use of fixed pitons or bolts and by placing your own protection devices, do not assume that there is adequate protection available higher just because the route protection rating indicates the route is not an "X" or an "R" rating. Every route is potentially an "X" (a fall may be deadly), due to the inherent hazards of climbing—including, for example, failure or absence of fixed protection, your own equipment's failure, or improper use of climbing equipment.

THERE ARE NO WARRANTIES, WHETHER EXPRESS OR IMPLIED, THAT THIS GUIDEBOOK IS ACCURATE OR THAT THE INFORMATION CONTAINED IN IT IS RELIABLE. THERE ARE NO WARRANTIES OF FITNESS FOR A PARTICULAR PURPOSE OR THAT THIS GUIDE IS MERCHANTABLE. YOUR USE OF THIS BOOK INDICATES YOUR ASSUMPTION OF THE RISK THAT IT MAY CONTAIN ERRORS AND IS AN ACKNOWLEDGMENT OF YOUR OWN SOLE RESPONSIBILITY FOR YOUR CLIMBING SAFETY.

ACKNOWLEDGMENTS

This book is dedicated to my good friends Fred and Richard Aschert. Thanks for all the wonderful times in the vertical world, past, present, and future.

A book of this scope would not be possible without the help and encouragement of many people. First, I would like to thank my wife Laurel for always being supportive and for constantly being there. With your love, everything is possible. To Stewart Green for his friendship and his considerable editing and photography skills—Stewart, you made this a better book, many thanks.

My thanks also go to the numerous climbing partners I have had the pleasure to rope up with in the Garden of the Gods, including Mark Rolofson, Peter Gallagher, Fred Aschert, Richard Aschert, Gene Smith, Ed Webster, Larry Kledzik, and Bob Robertson.

TABLE OF CONTENTS

GARDEN OF THE GODS LOCATOR MAP

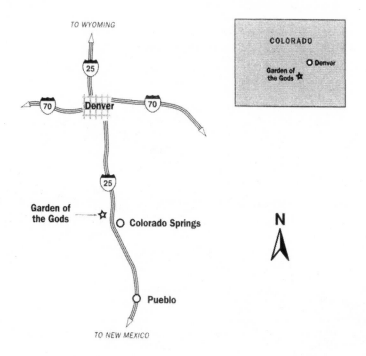

TOPO LEGEND

------------	Face climbing
—————	Chimney or crack
∘∘∘∘∘∘∘∘∘	Obscured route
Ⓧ	Fixed bolt or piton
Ⓧ	One-piece fixed anchor
ⓍⓍ	Two-piece fixed anchor
Ⓧ ⓍⓍ	Three-piece fixed anchor
•	Natural gear belay
150'	Descent route
11a	Difficulty rating
16	Route number

GARDEN OF THE GODS AREA MAP

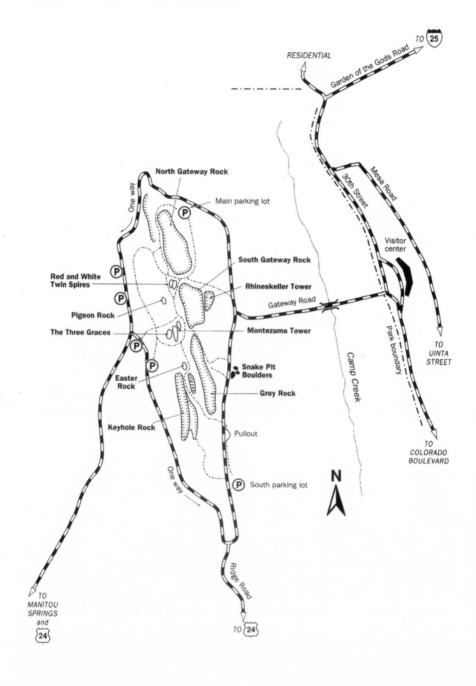

INTRODUCTION

Garden of the Gods

The Garden of the Gods, located on the west side of the sprawling front-range city of Colorado Springs, offers many unique face and crack climbs on towering rock formations of soft sandstone. Officially a Colorado Springs city park, Garden of the Gods is situated in a dramatic position against the foothills below 14,110-foot Pikes Peak, often called America's most famous mountain. The Garden is located at the southern foot of the Rampart Range.

The sandstone formations and towers in the Garden of the Gods are part of a series of exposed hogback ridges that extend from Fort Collins in northern Colorado to Canon City and Colorado City in the southern part of the state. Few places in Colorado offer the variety and age of the exposed rock, ranging from billion-year-old Pikes Peak granite to recent 50,000-year-old gravel deposits. Over the last 25 million years, the Garden's rock layers were uplifted and tilted

Garden of the Gods City Park. Stewart M. Green photo

as the Rocky Mountains rose to the west. Water and wind erosion did the rest of the sculpting, weathering the rock into dramatic formations that attract tourists, nature lovers, and rock climbers from around the world.

The climbing in the Garden of the Gods is different from other sandstone climbing areas. The rock is soft and varies in quality. Some of it has a hard, smooth veneer, while elsewhere it has the brittle consistency of dried brown sugar. Handholds found here include crisp fingertip edges, loose dinner-plate-sized flakes, huge potholes, small two-finger pockets, and straight-in cracks.

The routes range in height from 40 to 375 feet and from 1 to 8 pitches long. Most of the climbs are protected with soft angle pitons pounded into predrilled 3- to 5-inch-long holes in the soft sandstone. Bear in mind that most of the drilled pitons are at least 15 years old. They should be treated with caution and always backed up when possible, especially at belay and rappel stations.

Another unique characteristic of the Garden is the pronounced effect that rain and snow have on the rock. The soft sandstone should not be climbed on after periods of moisture such as severe rainstorms or heavy snowfalls. The rock becomes very fragile when it is wet, causing crucial holds to snap off and flakes to break. Such conditions can alter the climb and should be avoided at all costs. Several huge rockfalls occurred in May 1999 after a week of heavy rainfall, dramatically changing several routes. The rock surface is also very sandy after a rain. Many Garden climbers carry a small brush for sweeping sandy holds. Spring and summer are the most common times for heavy moisture. Winter snowstorms are usually dry and pose little danger to the rock, which usually dries out in a couple of days.

Here are some suggestions for visiting climbers: Don't add any fixed gear to pre-existing routes. Don't chop or remove any fixed gear on established climbs. Don't create or manufacture any holds, period! Don't litter. Pick up your own trash as well as that of inconsiderate tourists and climbers—it won't kill you. Trash cans are spaced along the tourist path through the main Garden zone. Climb clean, and leave no visible marks or offensively colored slings. Observe any posted raptor or other wildlife closures. These are usually on the east face of Grey Rock.

This guidebook does not include every single route in the Garden of the Gods. Some routes are just not worth doing. The bolt-ladder aid routes are omitted since they offer nothing more than a pull up on fixed pins.

GARDEN OF THE GODS CLIMBING REGULATIONS All climbers must register annually at the Garden of the Gods visitor center on 30th Street on the east side of the park. Go in before climbing and fill out a registration card and review the current regulations. The registration is good for one year.

The following is a brief description of the park rules:

Bob D'Antonio on The Extremist (5.12a), Grey Rock. STEWART M. GREEN PHOTO

- Only technical rock climbing and bouldering are permitted in the Garden of the Gods. Scrambling without ropes and sport rappelling are prohibited. Rappelling is allowed only in conjunction with technical climbing ascents. "Rock scrambling" is defined as climbing higher than 10 feet above the ground without using proper technical climbing equipment.

- The use of white chalk is not allowed in the park. Only approved colored substitutes can be used.

- Any slings left at belay and rappel anchors must match the color of the rock.

- Some routes or faces may be seasonally closed to climbing for nesting raptors.

- Night climbing or overnight bivouacking is not allowed on the cliffs. Climbers should plan and execute their climb during daylight hours.

- Climbers are asked not to climb on any formation that is wet or frosted. Climbing after rain, snow, and freezing temperatures hastens the deterioration of the sandstone.

- A registered adult climber must accompany all climbers under the age of 12.

- Okay, now go have some fun on some of the best sandstone routes in the country!

CLIMBING DANGERS AND SAFETY Whenever you lace up your climbing shoes and tie into the rope, you run the risk of getting hurt or, worse yet, killing yourself or your partner. Some of the routes in this guidebook are dangerous and should only be attempted by climbers certain of their ability to climb at the level of the route. Don't be fooled by the number grade. A 5.9 move on a sport route with a bolt at your face is way easier than a 5.9 move with your last piece of protection a distant 20 feet below your feet. Always climb safe and climb smart. If you have done most of your climbing inside a gym, you should limit your outside climbing to sport routes. Do not attempt to climb traditional routes without knowing how to properly place gear and set natural belays. Remember that every route, no matter how safe it seems or how much protection it has on it, is a potential nightmare. Respect the rock, the rating, and your abilities.

This guide gives you the most accurate information available on the Garden of the Gods routes. Once you reach the base of your chosen route, it is your responsibility to take care of your partner and yourself. If a climb looks too hard, don't do it. If a climb looks too runout, don't do it. Ratings are very subjective and should always be taken with a grain of salt. Again, a 5.10 route with four bolts in 20 feet is much different from a 5.10 route with natural gear every 15 feet. If you are just learning how to climb, hook up with a competent guide or a more experienced partner. You will learn more in one day with a skilled climber than you could ever learn in a month on your own.

When you're climbing, self-preservation always comes first. If you are feeling weak, go climb something easy. If you are planning to solo a route, do it alone and away from people. They don't want to see your mangled body at the bottom of the cliff. Always use common sense and remember that good judgment will save your life. Bad judgment will kill you and ruin someone else's day.

STAR RATING A route may have one to three stars following the rating. This indicates the quality of the route. One star represents good, with three stars being a route of outstanding quality.

ETHICS Almost all of the climbs in this book were established between 1960 and 1990. Most of these routes were first done with traditional methods, from the ground up with natural gear or drilled pitons that were placed for protection on the lead. Please respect the accomplishments of the first ascent party by not adding bolts to existing routes. If a bolt needs to be replaced, ask for permission from the first ascent party. Too many climbers in the Colorado Springs area have taken it upon themselves to change routes without asking. Don't be one of them. If you are trying to do a route and it is too hard, don't change the character of the route by chipping or altering holds—just work at getting better. A traditional climb with hard moves and difficult gear placements should be left as a testimony to each climber's ability to successfully climb the route.

Chipping and altering routes, especially on established routes, not only degrades the first ascent effort, it also degrades climbing itself. Most climbers don't care if you hang, grab a sling, or fall 100 times on a route. But climbers do care if you change the route by altering the rock or the protection.

In the end, how you ascend the rock is more important than reaching the top of the route. Take pride in the style in which you climb. If you're a sport climber, don't chip a route just to make it easier. Take your frustrations to the gym and work out to be stronger and more skilled. If you find a blank piece of sandstone, don't chip holds in it. Instead, look a little harder and perhaps you'll find just enough holds to make it go.

What we do today affects what will happen tomorrow. Each of us is leaving a legacy for future climbers to follow. Learn about our sport. Search out and read about the history of the climbing area. Not only will it give you a historical perspective, it will also enhance your visit. Also work to keep our crags open to public use by joining the Access Fund. Get involved in access issues on a local level. You can make a difference. What all climbers need to realize is that the rock is not an infinite resource. There is only so much rock available to practice our vertical art. Every time you go climbing, respect the rock as well as the privilege and the responsibilities that come with climbing it.

Fred Aschert on Cowboy Boot Crack (5.7), North Gateway Rock. STEWART M. GREEN PHOTO

RATING SYSTEM This guide uses the Yosemite Decimal System (YDS), the system that most American climbers are familiar with. The routes in the Garden of the Gods range in difficulty from 5.0 to 5.13. A 5.10 slab route could be easier or harder than a 5.10 crack. Use the rating system with a grain of salt; routes at the same grade can be completely different. An R or an X after the grade of a route denotes added danger and requires that the climber should be competent at or above the level of the route to safely ascend it. An R- or X-rated climb means that there is little or no protection and that a fall could cause serious injury or death. Remember that all climbs are R or X rated, depending on weather conditions, missing fixed gear, or your abilities on any given day.

Some routes have a (+) or (-). This subgrade only means that the route is either easy (-) or hard (+). To further confuse you, many routes have a letter subgrade of a, b, c, or d. These subgrades are used to fine-tune the rating of routes that are 5.10 or harder. A 5.10a is a lot less difficult than a 5.10d. Most routes are rated by the most difficult move on the climb. Hence a climb with a single move of 5.11 may feel easier than a climb with many sustained moves of 5.10.

The majority of the routes in the Garden of the Gods are equipped with fixed gear including drilled pitons and bolts. These require very little natural gear to safely protect them. It is, however, a good idea to carry extra slings for tying off potholes as well as some natural gear like Friends or Tri-cams for added protection.

Ian Spencer-Green bouldering at The Blowouts, a popular area on North Gateway Rock. STEWART M. GREEN PHOTO

CLIMBING HISTORY The Garden of the Gods is one of the oldest climbing areas in the United States. The great American climbing pioneer Albert Ellingwood was the first person to climb technical routes in the Garden. Ellingwood, a Rhodes scholar and Colorado College professor, brought proper climbing techniques back from England and introduced them to Colorado's crags. Considering the soft rock and his crude climbing gear, his ascents in the 1920s are nothing short of amazing. His protégé Bob Ormes also established routes in the Garden in the 1920s and 1930s. In the 1940s, Vernon Twombly and Stanley Boucher, armed with better equipment, climbed several classics including the popular Practice Slab on South Gateway Rock. The 1950s brought Harvey Carter, whose innovative use of drilled angles allowed the development of some of today's classics. Army climbers from nearby Fort Carson also did ascents of some moderate routes including Montezuma Tower, West Point Crack, and The Three Graces.

The late 1960s and early 1970s were the heyday of Garden rock climbing. In the 1960s, the great climber Layton Kor made several trips down from Boulder and put up some hard aid routes including *Anaconda* and *Kor's Korner.* The 1970s brought modern free climbing to the Garden, with many hard routes accomplished in a clean style. Some of the leading activists included Jim Dunn, Earl Wiggins, Ed Webster, Steve Hong, and Leonard Coyne. Difficult routes such as *Anaconda, Amazing Grace, Cocaine,* and *Pipe Dreams* were just a few of the great routes done by these outstanding climbers. Not only did Garden climbers establish outstanding local routes; their accomplishments in the world of climbing are mind-boggling. Dunn, one of America's finest free climbers, added many hard first ascents around the United States, and his solo first ascent of a new route on El Capitan in Yosemite rocked the climbing world in the early 1970s. Wiggins, known for bold leads and ropeless ascents of many hard climbs, was the first person to free-solo the *Scenic Cruise* in the Black Canyon—and he did it in 3 hours. Back in 1976 this was a bold and brilliant ascent and, even by today's standards, is an audacious and reckless undertaking. Coyne's first free ascent of the Forrest-Walker route (*Stratosfear* 5.11+ R/X) in the Black Canyon was a bold undertaking, and to this day the route has seen few ascents. Webster, a New Englander and student at Colorado College, has put up first ascents around the world, including the first ascent of a new route on Mount Everest.

The 1980s brought a new group of climbers that wanted to leave their mark on Garden climbing. And, judging by the sheer number of first ascents from that period, they did. Bob Robertson, Peter Gallagher, Mark Rolofson, Fred and Richard Aschert, Larry Kledzik, and Bob D'Antonio put up many excellent routes, including *Men at Work, Horribly Heinous,* and *The Refugee.* D'Antonio, Aschert, and Rolofson were particularly active, adding over 50 new routes between them.

Earl Wiggins finds a Place in the Sun (5.8), Finger Face, North Gateway Rock. STEWART M. GREEN PHOTO

The early 1990s brought an interest in modern sport routes. Ric Giemen went to work on the east face of Grey Rock and added several routes, with *Diesel and Dust* and *Civil Disobedience* being the best. The future potential for routes in the Garden of the Gods is, however, severely limited. Since all the best routes have been climbed here, what the future holds for the Garden is hard to predict. But one thing is for sure: The Garden of the Gods is simply one of the most unique and beautiful climbing areas in the United States.

HOW TO GET THERE The Garden of the Gods city park is located on the west side of Colorado Springs. There are several ways to access the park. The best is from the east via 30th Street. Reach 30th Street from the north by exiting Interstate 25 onto Garden of the Gods Road. Drive west on the busy street until it dead-ends at 30th Street. Turn left and follow 30th Street to Garden Drive, opposite the park visitor center. Garden Drive can also be reached from the south from Colorado Avenue and U.S. Highway 24.

Go west on Garden Drive to the one-way Garden loop drive. Go right on the one-way road and proceed to a large parking lot at the northeast corner of North Gateway Rock. This is the best parking area for climbers. Other parking areas are on the west side of the loop road, west of the rock formations. Another large parking area on the south side of the park is a good place to park for climbing at Grey Rock and Keyhole Rock.

A paved visitor trail leaves the main parking area at North Gateway Rock and runs between North and South Gateway Rocks. It then splits and makes a loop through the main Garden zone. This trail is the best way to access routes on North and South Gateway Rocks, Montezuma Tower, and the Three Graces, as well as Grey Rock and Keyhole Rock farther south.

Garden of the Gods.

North Gateway Rock

South Gateway Rock

White and Red
Twin Spires

Grey Rock

Montezuma
Tower

The
Three
Graces

Keyhole Rock

CHAPTER ONE

North Gateway Rock

North Gateway Rock, the largest rock formation in the. Garden of the Gods, offers some of the park's best quality sandstone, as well as a concentration of face climbing routes up to 8 pitches long. Many of the area's classics are found on this complex formation.

The best parking area for North Gateway is at the main visitor parking lot at the northeast corner of the formation. From 30th Street and the visitor center, drive on the main park road and go right on the one-way road. Park at the large, obvious parking lot on the left. The Tower of Babel routes are approached from a cliff-base trail that begins on the west side of the parking lot. The rest of the routes are approached via the paved trail that begins on the south side of the lot. Walk south on the trail past the East Face routes (Route 54 to Route 57) to the Gateway between North and South Gateway Rocks. Go right on a paved trail here. This trail heads northwest below the Finger Face, the Cowboy Boot Face, and the West Face. Routes are described counterclockwise beginning with the northern routes on the Tower of Babel.

Descent Routes: There are two major descent routes off North Gateway Rock. The Tourist Gully runs along the base of the Finger Face from the south end of the rock to a prominent notch at the top. It offers easy assess to the Finger Face routes and is the usual descent route for all West Face routes that finish at the top of the rock. The city of Colorado Springs has installed huge eyebolts in the gully to assist in rescues. The eyebolts are convenient rappel anchors for climbers descending the gully.

The East Ledges, a complex system of narrow, exposed ledges on North Gateway's east face, start above the paved trail below *Max's Mayhem*'s obvious crack system at the southeast corner of the formation. This ledge system offers access to several routes.

The descent route from the Tower of Babel is via Hidden Valley, a hidden sandstone canyon behind the Tower of Babel. Eye-bolt anchors are found on its

Bob D'Antonio on Mr. Fred (5.10d), North Gateway Rock. STEWART M. GREEN PHOTO

east side, making it possible to rappel 150 feet to the ground. There are a number of rescues on the East Ledges every year, with tourists being the main culprits. The ledges are exposed, narrow, scary, and tend to ice up in cold weather.

Tower of Babel

This sheer, north-facing tower lies at the northern end of North Gateway Rock. The triple-summited tower looms over the main visitor parking lot at the northeast corner of North Gateway. *Anaconda*, a spectacular 3-pitch crack route up an overhanging face, ascends the right-hand tower. Access all the routes by parking at the main lot and following a trail to the base of the formation. Routes are described left to right.

1   **North End Chimney (6 R)**   2 pitches. The name explains the kind of climbing found on this route which ascends the prominent, deep chimney that separates the East and Middle Towers. The face climbing on the first pitch is the crux and has the least protection. **Gear:** Friends to #4, nuts, and slings. FA: Stanley Boucher and Vernon Twombly, 1947.

2   **Triple Exposure (12d)** ★★   4 pitches. The hardest route in the Garden. This sustained route has seen very few complete, all-free ascents. The line ascends the obvious, intermittent, crack line up the northeast face of the Middle Tower of Babel. Expect excellent thin crack climbing with good bolt and gear protection. **Pitch 1:** Climb the first 30' of the *North End Chimney*, angle right past a drilled piton on sandy holds to a line of 10 bolts right of a shallow groove. Face climb up the bolt ladder (5.11d) and step right at the top to a hanging belay from 2 fixed pitons. **Pitch 2:** Crank up a thin crack (crux 5.12c/d) past 4 bolts to a hanging belay from 2 drilled pitons. **Pitch 3:** Continue straight up the crack system (5.10d) and, where it ends, step left (5.11b) into a right-facing corner with 2 bolts to a 2-fixed-piton belay stance. **Pitch 4:** From the belay, angle right past several bolts to a steep crack and climb to the summit. **Descent:** Rappel from anchors into Hidden Valley and follow the East Ledges south to the top of Tourist Gully or rappel from Hidden Valley to the ground. **Gear:** Stoppers, Friends to #4, and many quickdraws. FA: Doug Snively and friends 1971. FFA: Richard Aschert, Will Gadd, and Dave Dangle, 1986.

3   **Anaconda (11)** ★★★   3 pitches. An old Kor aid route that is now one of the Garden's premier free climbs. This sustained classic offers laybacking, jamming, and exposed face climbing. Why drive to Moab when you can climb *Anaconda?* Begin on some boulders and ledges at the far right, northwest corner of the West Tower. **Pitch 1:** Layback up an expanding flake (5.9) and traverse left past a drilled angle into a vertical crack. Jam and face climb (5.10) up the crack to a 2-piton anchor at 60'. Work up the overhanging, left-facing corner above past some pitons to a 2-piton anchor on the left. Most parties

Tower of Babel.

rappel or lower 100' from here. **Pitch 2:** Climb up right along an overhanging off-width crack (5.10a) to a ledge with a 2-piton anchor on the right. **Pitch 3:** Move up a shallow, left-facing corner (5.10b) and finish with runout face climbing to the tower summit. **Descent:** Make a 2-rope rappel south into Hidden Valley and another 2-rope rappel east to the base, just south of the main parking area. **Gear:** Friends to #4, stoppers, and RPs. FA: Layton Kor and Gary Ziegler, 1965. FFA: Earl Wiggins, Jim Dunn, and John Sherwood, 1975.

4   Tourist Trap Gully (7) 1 pitch. This obscure route tucked into Hidden Valley behind the Tower of Babel has seen many rescues. Although it is now illegal to scramble around up here without proper climbing equipment, tourists used to climb down the chimney but were unable to scale back up its smooth surface.

5   The Refugee (11+) ★★ 1 pitch. This route is somewhat hard to find, but the climbing is well worth the effort to locate it. The best approach to the route is via the East Ledges. Follow the East Ledges to Hidden Valley, a secret amphitheater that lies between the Tower of Babel and the North Buttress of North Gateway Rock. The route ascends the steep slab right of Tourist Trap Gully. Face climb up a short corner and edge past some fixed gear (5.11d). At the third pin, traverse left (5.11a) and climb straight up past 3 more fixed pins (5.10b) to a crack finish. Belay and rappel from a 2-piton anchor. **Gear:** Stoppers, quickdraws, and long slings for potholes. FA: Mark Rolofson and Bob D'Antonio, 1983.

6   South Ridge of Tower of Babel (8) 1 pitch. A short, spectacular pitch to the airy top of a sandstone tower. Access the route from the East Ledges to Hidden Valley. Follow a line of 4 fixed pins up the south ridge of the tower. **Gear:** Quickdraws. FA: U.S. Army climbers, circa 1945.

7   Water Crack (9+) 1 pitch. This route is on the far north side of the west face of North Gateway Rock. It climbs an obvious water groove/crack system to a notch just south of the West Tower of Babel. It is seldom climbed. 2 fixed pins. **Gear:** Bring a selection of stoppers, hexes, and Friends. FA: Earl Wiggins and John Sherwood, 1975.

The West Face

8   Touchy Situation (11c/d) ★★ 7 pitches. Lots of sustained face climbing. The route takes a wild line up across the beautiful, upper west face of North Gateway Rock above the giant overhang. Scary exposure make this route a rarely climbed Garden climb. Start the route by climbing *Rainbow Bridge* and the first and second pitches of *Over the Rainbow.* **Pitch 4:** Traverse left (5.11a) from the belay past 6 pins to a 2-piton belay. **Pitch 5:** Follow a line of fixed pins straight up (5.10c) to a 2-piton belay. **Pitch 6:** Continue straight up (5.11c/d

North Gateway Rock—West Face.

crux) to Vine Ledge. **Pitch 7:** Edge up (5.10b) past 3 fixed pitons to the top of the formation. **Gear:** 16 quickdraws and #3 Friend. FA: Richard Aschert and Scott Szcymak, 1985.

VARIATION: Wimpish and Weak (10d) Go left from the belay before the crux pitch (5.10d) and escape to an easier gully.

8.5   Arching Crack (6)   1 pitch. This route follows a long crack that arches under the large overhang above and left of the Blowouts bouldering area to a 2-bolt anchor in the middle of the crack. For some strange reason this traversing route is quite popular. **Descent:** Rappel to the ground from the anchors. **Gear:** Friends, nuts, and slings. FA: Unknown.

9   Grapefruit Dance (12a) ★★   1 pitch. This fun sport route ascends the left side of the overhanging wall of North Gateway West Face, just left of the Blowouts bouldering area. Make a series of difficult, gymnastic moves past 4 drilled pitons to a 2-piton anchor. FA: Will Gadd, 1988.

10   Over the Rainbow (11a) ★★   4 pitches. This route offers great position and good climbing on somewhat loose rock. Climb *Rainbow Bridge* to the first belay. **Pitch 1:** Traverse left (5.8) above the huge overhang to a 2-piton belay. 3 drilled pitons. **Pitch 2:** Continue left (5.10c) past 7 fixed pins to a 2-piton belay just above the lip of the overhang. **Pitch 3:** Edge straight up past a ladder of 11 fixed pins (5.11a to the big pothole and 5.9 above) to Vine Ledge and belay.

Pitch 4: Scramble right on the crack ledge and climb *Pot of Gold,* a 5.8 face pitch with 2 drilled pins, to the summit of the rock. **Descent:** Scramble down ledges to the left onto a big ledge. Walk south and downclimb Tourist Gully. **Gear:** 15 quickdraws. FA: Ed Webster, Bryan Becker, and Leonard Coyne, 1978.

11   Rainbow Bridge (11a) ★★   1 pitch. This route has great climbing, but watch out for the runout getting to the belay ledge. Start by jamming a short 5.6 crack up a pillar. Face climb steep rock above through a series of sandy potholes to a spacious ledge with a 2-piton belay/rappel anchor. **Descent:** Make a double-rope rappel to the ground. **Gear:** Quickdraws and #3 Friend. FA: Ed Webster and Peter Mayfield, 1979.

12   Borghoff's Blunder (10) ★   3 pitches. A pretty good route for being a blunder! The crux is a well-protected mantle move over a bulge. Most parties rap after the first (crux) pitch since the upper pitches are loose. Jam a nice crack (5.6) up a pillar. Step up right and edge onto a face. Make the crux mantle (5.10b) at a piton (easy A0 if you stand on the pin!). Work up left along potholes to a 2-piton belay/rappel ledge with a juniper. **Descent:** Make a double-rope rappel to the ground. **Gear:** Some small cams, #3 and #3.5 Friends, and quickdraws. FA: Michael Borghoff, 1960. FFA: Steve Cheyney and Peter Croff, 1960s.

13   Henry the Pig (8) 1 pitch. Don't get a ticket climbing this route. Named after the policeman who ticketed the first ascent party for an illegal parking job.

North Gateway Rock—West Face.

This single pitch route starts on Hollywood Ledge on the upper face. Access it by climbing *Borgoff's Blunder's* first 2 pitches to the crack ledge. Go left on the ledge from the second belay on *Borgoff's* and face climb past 4 fixed pins to a belay on Vine Ledge. Finish up *Vine Ledge Exit* above. FA: Leonard Coyne, Ed Bailey, and Mark Rolofson, 1976.

14   Vine Ledge Exit (8) 1 pitch. A short, exit pitch off Vine Ledge and the logical finish to *Henry the Pig.* Vine Ledge is a long ledge that runs along the upper part of the West face of North Gateway Rock. Fun, airy moves past 3 drilled pitons to the summit. FA: Unknown.

16   Pot of Gold (8) ★★ 1 pitch. Is there really a pot of gold at the end of a rainbow? Do the route and find out. From the left edge of Vine Ledge climb a face past 2 fixed pins to the top. FA: Ed Webster and Peter Mayfield, 1978.

17   Squids in Bondage (8 R) 1 pitch. This is a runout pitch that goes up and right from the first belay ledge on *Borgoff's Blunder* past 4 fixed pins to a large ledge. FA: Ed Webster, Leonard Coyne, Wendy White, and Mike Heintz, 1977.

18   Men at Work (11) ★★★ 2 pitches. This route is a genuine Garden classic. The full-body lunge crux (can also be done static) on the first pitch will keep you on your toes and your body off the rock. **Pitch 1:** Climb the first 10' of the *Borgoff's Blunder* crack, then move right up a steep face past several potholes and 5 fixed pins to a 2-piton belay. **Pitch 2:** Continue straight up past 5 fixed pins to a 2-piton belay. These pitches can be combined into a single lead. **Descent:** Rappel 130 feet with 2 ropes to the ground. FA: Bob D'Antonio and Mark Rolofson, 1983.

19   Pete and Bob's (11b/c) ★★ 4 pitches. The first pitch is a popular classic. A 1999 rockfall, however, dramatically altered this pitch making it dangerous and loose. Use caution. **Pitch 1:** Climb up and left to gain the crack. Jam and face climb past some fixed pins to a 2-piton belay atop a big flake. Most parties rappel 75' from here. **Pitch 2:** Dance across a thin face, traversing up and right on loose and ever-changing edges. Pull down on fragile holds, not out. Belay on a small ledge with pitons. **Pitch 3:** Pull over a bulge above the belay and climb to a 2-bolt anchor on a small stance on the upper slab. **Pitch 4:** Climb a poorly protected slab (5.6 R) with 2 bad pitons to the top of the face. **Descend** down the Tourist Gully. FA: Peter Croft and Bob Stauch, 1960s. FFA (Pitch 1): Steve Cheyney, 1960s. FFA (whole route): Kurt Rasmussen, 1973.

20   Pete and Bob's Face (9 R) ★ 1 pitch. This is a loose face route with 4 widely spaced pitons that starts just right of *Pete and Bob's.* End at the 2-piton anchor atop the flake.

21   Horribly Heinous (12a) ★★ 1 pitch. You won't wait in line for this one! Great moves and hard climbing with protection from some old pins of dubious quality. The first ascent of this route was a real breakthrough in Garden standards. This single-pitch route starts 75' right of *Pete and Bob's* and ascends a steep face past 9 fixed pins to a 2-piton belay. **Descent:** Rappel 85' from the belay to the ground. FA: Bob D'Antonio and Mark Rolofson, 1983.

22   Indecent Exposure (7 R) ★ 2 pitches. This once popular route is now seldom climbed because of poor and sparse fixed protection. Take extreme care when climbing it not to pull out any more of the pro!! The route would become popular again if it were retrobolted with modern bolt protection. Bring prusik loops. A fall from the overhang on pitch 1 would result in the climber dangling freely 150' above the ground. The start is hard to find. Access it from Tourist Gully by scrambling up the gully until you're just past Tweedledumshire Spire. Climb jugs up the left wall to a ridge and scramble down an exposed ridge to a notch behind the spire. Rappel 50' from an anchor to an exposed belay stance with pitons or belay from *Amazing Grace*'s chain anchor. Use caution and a rope when accessing this route. **Pitch 1:** From the anchors atop *Amazing Grace*, traverse up left 50' on flakes to an inside corner. Move up left around the corner to a hidden piton in a pothole. Follow good holds along the lip of the exposed overhang and work up left along a seam (5.7 R) to a narrow ramp and a 2-piton anchor. **Pitch 2:** Edge up loose flakes on the slab above (5.6 R) past a couple of funky fixed pitons. **Descent:** Scramble around and descend Tourist Gully. **Gear:** Tri-cams and quickdraws. FA: Richard Cole and others, 1965.

23   Amazing Grace (11d R) ★★ 1 pitch. This Wiggins classic starts 200' down right of *Horribly Heinous* below a steep face and right of a cave. Climb up right of a large pothole to a fixed pin and a hard mantle move. Crank the crux mantle (5.11d R) and edge straight up on flexible flakes to a 2-piton chain belay. 12 fixed pitons. **Descent:** Rappel 85' to the ground. The route used to feature long runouts on the less than solid rock. The runouts have since been mitigated with the replacement of some fixed pins, taking away the first ascent's bold lead. FA: Earl Wiggins, Leonard Coyne, and Ed Webster, 1977.

24   Saving Grace (9+ R) 1 pitch. An obscure route. This route climbs the first 75' of *Amazing Grace* before veering left at bolt 11. Traverse up left across an unprotected face to a small overhang. Work past the overhang (5.9+) to *Indecent Exposure*'s traverse. 4 fixed pitons. Finish up *Indecent Exposure*. FA: Ed Webster and Leonard Coyne, 1977.

25   Escape Gully (10a) 1 pitch. A finishing pitch to *Amazing Grace*. Starts at the *Amazing Grace* chain belay. From the belay, traverse up left on easy rock to the base of a steep right-facing gully. Climb the gully to the top of the ridge west of the Tourist Gully. **Gear:** Medium Friends and nuts. FA: Harrison Dekker and Sue Patenade, 1982.

North Gateway Rock—West Face.

26   Fall from Grace (10b R) ★ 2 pitches. Make sure you say your prayers. A fall in certain places could leave the leader in an uncomfortable position.,The route climbs to the summit of Tweedledumshire Spire, a semidetached pinnacle. Reach the start of the route by climbing *Unzipped* (Route 29) and belaying from a 2-piton anchor. **Pitch 1:** Traverse up left (5.10b) along a break at the base of the spire. 4 fixed pitons. Belay at the chain anchors atop *Amazing Grace.* **Pitch 2:** Expect some tricky route-finding and devious protection. Climb up right past some potholes (5.10b) on the steep west face of the spire to a 2-piton belay stance. Belay here or continue (5.9) to the summit of the spire. **Descent:** Rappel into Tourist Gully and scramble down. **Gear:** Friends, Tricams, and quickdraws. FA (Pitch 1): Leonard Coyne and Ed Webster, 1977. FA (Pitch 2): Leonard Coyne, Ed Webster, and Ed Russell, 1977.

27   The Warren Route (10d R) 1 pitch. Say even more prayers. Good face climbing but very long runouts on somewhat fragile rock.You could hit the deck if you blow the second clip at the crux. Best to toprope this one! Begin below the Cowboy Boot Face and right of *Amazing Grace.* Edge up the steep wall using thin flakes and edges past 4 drilled pitons to a 2-piton rappel anchor. **Descent:** Rappel 100' to the ground. FA: Robert Warren and Mike Johnson, 1983.

28   The Zipper (11d) ★★ 3 pitches. An old aid route that now goes free up the impressive southwest face of Tweedledumshire Spire. In its present state the route offers some good moves and excellent exposure. Some bolts may be loose. It would be a classic if it were rebolted. **Pitch 1:** Start 50' right of the *Warren Route.* Climb *Unzipped,* a nice face with 3 fixed pins to a 2-piton anchor (top of *Warren Route*). Clip into the anchor and climb up right 30' to a 2-eyebolt belay at the upper right base of Tweedledumshire Spire. **Pitch 2:** Traverse left a few feet to the start of the bolt ladder. Climb past 9 bolts and fixed pitons (5.11d) to a belay from 2 fixed pins. **Pitch 3:** Go right and up past 2 fixed pins (5.9) to the top of the spire. **Descent:** Rappel into the Tourist Gully. **Gear:** Friends #3, #3.5, and #4, and quickdraws. FA: Gary Zeigler and John Auld, 1965. FFA: Mark Rolofson and Jeff Britt, 1984.

Cowboy Boot Face

This popular, southwest-facing, 100-foot-high face stands just left of Tourist Gully and below Tweedledumshire Spire. Reach the base of the face by scrambling up easy rock to a large, flat terrace. All the described routes end at belay/rappel anchors. Use carabiners on the anchors for toproping to avoid wearing out the fixed anchors. Routes are described from left to right.

29   Unzipped (7) ★ A popular and fun outing. From the terrace, climb up left past 3 drilled pitons to a 2-piton anchor.

North Gateway Rock—Cowboy Boot Face.

30   Trigger Finger (10b R) ★ 1 pitch. This route has excellent face and crack climbing with great protection. The route starts 10' right of *Unzipped*. Climb 35' with no pro to the first piton. Edge up flakes and edges (5.10b) past several more fixed pins to a 2-eyebolt belay below the spire. 5 fixed pitons. **Descent:** Rappel 100' with double ropes. FA: Dirk Tyler and Dave Hodges, 1979.

31   Fastest Drill (9) 1 pitch. From the third piton on *Trigger Finger*, step left past 2 more pins to the eyebolt belay. **Descent:** Rappel 100' with double ropes. FA: Ed Webster, Mack Johnson, and Dave Sweet, 1978.

32 Cowboy Boot Crack (6) ★★★ 1 pitch. This moderate route is extremely popular and for good reason—it is one of the best easy routes in the Garden. Start on the large sandstone terrace below the face and left of the gully. Climb to a crack (large stopper) below the Cowboy Boot Flake. Step left and edge to an old, bent piton. Continue up the perfect crack, keeping left at the top to a 2-ring bolt anchor, 100'. It's possible at the top of the crack to move right onto a narrow ledge and tie-off a large horn for an anchor. **Descent:** Rappel 100' with double ropes. **Gear:** Large stopper, TCUs, small to medium Friends, and quickdraws. FA: Unknown, 1960s.

The Finger Face

This southwest-facing wall provides a number of well-protected, high-angle face climbs on edges and flakes that vary from very solid to very loose. The wall sees a lot of climbing traffic, particularly in the winter due to its sunny exposure. Remember, when climbing on the looser holds—pull down, not out! All of the routes are protected with fixed pitons and bolts unless otherwise noted. The routes on the face vary from well-protected, one-pitch routes to three-pitch horror shows with scant protection. Lots of fixed protection is found on the routes near *Mr. Fred*. Several routes either converge or crisscross each other in this general area. Study the topos carefully to figure out the lines. Use good judgment when climbing on this popular face.

Routes are described from left to right beginning at the top of the Tourist Gully, the large slashing gully that forms the base of the face.

33   Bald but Hairy (9+) 1 pitch. This short pitch starts in the Tourist Gully just below the Kissing Camel formation. 3 drilled pitons to 1-piton anchor. **Descent:** Rappel 50' from single anchor or traverse left (5.6) with no pro to gully (recommended). FA: Gary and Mark Hopkin, 1978.

34   Yellow Sunshine (9 R) 1 pitch. Start 25' right of *Bald but Hairy*. Climb up a shallow, right-facing corner past 2 fixed pins to a 1-bolt anchor. 2 drilled pitons to 1-piton anchor (same as Route 33). **Descent:** Rappel 50' from single anchor or traverse left (5.6) with no pro to gully (recommended). FA: Scott Szcymak, 1985.

North Gateway Rock—Finger Face.

35   Mr. Fred (10d) ★★ 2 pitches. This route offers reasonable protection and thought-provoking moves. It's named after Fred Aschert, an old Garden local. The route begins near the top of the gully. **Pitch 1:** Belay at a small pothole thread. Move out right to the first drilled piton and then climb thin edges past 3 more fixed pins to a 2-piton anchor. **Descent:** Rappel or lower 70'. **Pitch 2:** Continue face climbing up the slab above to a steep headwall and a 2-drilled piton anchor. 7 drilled pitons. **Descent:** Make a 2-rope, 165' rappel back to the gully. FA: Richard Aschert and Fred Aschert, 1984.

36   Pig Dreams (10c) ★★★ 2 pitches. Another classic Garden route. It's a hard tick if you're not great at smearing! This route takes a face line from Tourist Gully to an anchor near the top of the face. Begin down from *Mr. Fred.* **Pitch 1:** Climb a seam up left to the first pin. Make delicate traversing moves up right onto a sloping shelf. A thin face move off the right side leads to a good flake and a 2-bolt anchor. A 5.10 variation edges up from the left side of the shelf. **Pitch 2:** Face climb up right over a steeper headwall (5.10b) to the upper slab and a 2-piton belay/rappel anchor. 6 drilled pitons. **Descent:** Rappel the route. FA: Peter Gallagher and Fred Aschert, 1981.

37   Chatters (9+) ★★ 1 pitch. Another classic but has some loose flakes on the first section. Begin below a small roof and a left-angling seam. Climb flakes past 2 pins to the roof. Crank over the right side of the roof (5.9+) and follow the seam up left to a final, delicate, leftward traverse and a 2-drilled-piton anchor (same as *Pig Dreams*). 5 drilled pitons to 2-piton anchor. **Descent:** Rappel 70' to the gully. FA: Bob Robertson, Bob D'Antonio, and Larry Kledzik, 1982.

38   Fatal Curiosity (11 R/X) 1 pitch. A short, dangerous pitch that begins at *Pig Dreams's* first belay stance. From the belay, clip the first fixed pin on the second pitch of *Pig Dreams* and then go left. Run it out to a fixed piton below a roof, regroup, and run it out up and over the roof to a fixed pin and the 2-piton belay at the top of *Pig Dreams.* **Descent:** Rappel 150' to the Tourist Gully. Be prepared for long runouts between protection. **Gear:** 2.5 Tri-cam. FA: Richard Aschert, 1985.

39   Dancing in Swineland (10d) ★★ 2 pitches. Can pigs dance? Climb it and find out! Climb the first 2 pitches of *Dust to Dust* (Route 43). Angle left at the upper belay and follow a line of 6 fixed pins over a small overhang (5.10a) to a 2-piton belay at the top of *Pig Dreams's* second pitch. Traverse up left from the belay across *Mr. Fred* and continue left and up to crux flakes (5.10d) and a ledge with a 2-piton belay. **Descent:** 2 rappels to Tourist Gully. **Gear:** 14 quickdraws. FA: Pete Williams and Pete Gallagher, 1979.

40   Skip It or Clip It (11a) 1 pitch. This extremely well-protected route follows a long line of drilled pins. Start down right from *Chatters.* Face climb past 14 drilled pitons, skipping any you don't want to clip, to a final runout to a 2-drilled-piton anchor. **Gear:** 15 quickdraws. FA: Fred Aschert and Chuck Dagmen, 1989.

Emily Danti on Chatters (5.9). STEWART M. GREEN PHOTO

41   Triple Twilight (11a R) 2 pitches. A good route that has some runout sections. Start down right of Route 40. **Pitch 1:** Some thin, tricky face climbing (5.11a) leads past 4 drilled pitons to a 2-piton anchor. **Pitch 2:** Continue straight up past 4 drilled pins to a 2-piton belay on *Dust to Dust.* **Descent:** Rappel the route. FA: Bob Robertson and Carrie Robertson, 1988.

42   No Ethics Required (10d) ★ 1 pitch. It sounds like a Shelf Road route name. The rating of this thin edging testpiece yo-yos from easy 5.10 to hard 5.10 depending on what holds have broken off in the last thunderstorm! Belay in the middle of the Tourist Gully with Friends or Tri-cams in pockets for anchors. Climb directly up the steep face to the crux moves above a shallow pothole. 5 drilled pitons. **Descent:** Rappel or lower 70' to the gully. FA: Dave Bowmen and Bob Robertson, 1980.

43   Dust to Dust (10a R) ★★ 3 pitches. A classic route but not often done. **Pitch 1:** Climb *No Ethics Required* to its 2-piton belay anchor. **Pitch 2:** Climb easily up left past 2 drilled pins. Pull up the steeper wall above past 4 pins and step right to a 2-drilled-piton belay. **Pitch 3:** Move up left and crank past several potholes (Tri-cams) over a bulge to anchors on a ledge. **Descent:** Rappel 150' with double ropes to the Tourist Gully. **Gear:** Medium-size nuts or Tri-cams for potholes on the last pitch. FA: Kim Rodgers and Gary Isaacs, 1973.

44   Pete and Pete's (10 R) ★ 1 pitch. Be prepared for loose rock and long runouts on this upper face route. From the second belay of *Dust to Dust,* move right on loose flakes, then straight up to a belay ledge. 5 fixed pitons. **Descent:** Walk off down the East Ledges to the ground or make a double-rope, 165' rappel to the ground from the top of *Tidrick's* (Route 45). FA: Pete Williams and Peter Gallagher, 1979.

45   Son of Tidrick's to Tidrick's (8) ★★ 2 pitches. Most parties just do the first short pitch and lower. Start by belaying at a large eyebolt in the gully. **Pitch 1:** A fun 45' lead. Delicate moves lead up and right (5.8) to anchors on a small stance. 3 drilled pitons to 2-piton anchor. **Pitch 2:** The second pitch is *Tidrick's.* Climb crisp edges past 3 drilled pitons and make an obvious but easy (5.6) traverse right past 1 more pin to a 2-drilled-piton anchor with chains. **Descent:** Rappel 85' back to the belay or rappel 165' with double ropes to the base of the gully. FA: Leonard Coyne and Gary Campbell, 1976.

46   Place in the Sun (8) ★★ 1 pitch. This excellent winter route is one of the most popular lines up the Finger Face. Belay at a large eyebolt midway up the Tourist Gully. Climb down from the belay and traverse right (5.7) past a couple of fixed pins to a seam. Work up the seam to a stance and mantle past a loose flake. Continue edging up the steep face above (5.8) past a couple of good bolts to anchors on a small stance. 3 drilled pitons and 2 bolts to a 2-piton anchor with chains. **Descent:** Rappel 85' back to the belay or rappel 165' with

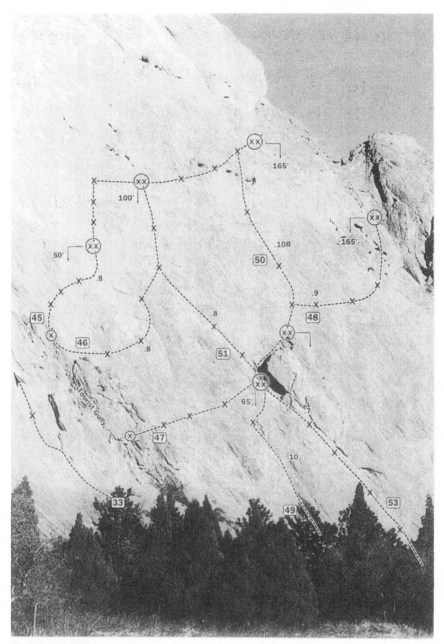

North Gateway Rock—Lower Finger Face.

double ropes to the base of the gully. FA: Ed Webster, Leonard Coyne, Kevin Murray, Bob Robertson, George Allen, Gary Hopkins, and Pete Williams, 1977.

47   Finger Traverse (7) ★★★ 1 pitch. This is one of the most frequented routes in the Garden and the site of many epics. It just might be the hardest 5.7 you'll every do! Start by scrambling up the Tourist Gully to a large eyebolt belay opposite the Finger. Traverse up and right to a belay alcove under the Finger, a small pillar. 3 bolts to a 2-drilled-piton anchor with chains. **Descent:** Rappel 65'. FA: Paul Radigen, Art Howells, John Auld, and Herby Hendricks, in the early 1960s.

48   Upper Finger Traverse (9) ★ 1 pitch. An old classic but now rarely climbed because the pitons are falling out. Use caution. Climb *Finger Traverse* to the belay alcove. Don't belay here but climb the groove above, up the left side of the Finger to a 2-drilled-piton belay ledge. Edge up and right across the steep, exposed slab past several old pins until it's possible to scramble up left in a fourth-class gully and a piton belay. **Descent:** Scramble onto a large ledge above the route and locate a 2-piton anchor on the far left side of the ledge. **Descent:** Make a 2-rope, 165' rappel to the base of the face. **Gear:** Bring small runners and Tri-cams for pothole pro. FA: Paul Radigen, Art Howells, John Auld, and Herby Hendricks, in the early 1960s.

49   Lower Finger Direct (10 TR) ★ An excellent toprope workout to do after climbing *Finger Traverse*. Face climb along a thin seam to the belay alcove at the base of the Finger.

Martha Morris on Finger Traverse (5.7), one of the most popular routes in the Garden. STEWART M. GREEN PHOTO

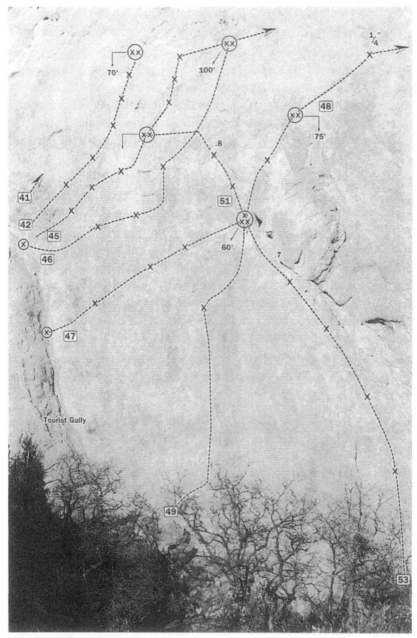

North Gateway Rock—Finger Face.

50   Upper Finger Direct (10 R/X) Another old classic that is seldom climbed because of general looseness and poor protection. It's best to toprope it from the ledge anchors at the top of the wall.

51   Tidrick's (8 R) ★★ 3 pitches. An old-style route that zigzags up the face and a must-do classic for the Garden freak. **Pitch 1:** Climb *Finger Traverse* (5.7) to the belay alcove. 3 bolts. **Pitch 2:** Fun climbing leads up left along a ramp to a dicey move over a headwall. Traverse out left (5.8) from the ramp above to a 2-drilled-piton anchor (top of *Son of Tidrick's to Tidrick's*). 3 bolts. **Pitch 3:** Edge up flakes above (5.7) to an obvious traverse that leads right to *Place in the Sun's* anchors. Belay here or continue up right on flexible flakes (5.8) past a couple fixed pins to a 2-drilled-piton anchor on a spacious ledge. **Descent:** Make a double-rope, 165' rappel down the face. FA: Rick Tidrick and company, 1960.

52   Psychic Grandma (9 R) ★ 5 to 6 pitches. An exciting girdle traverse of the Finger Face. The climb takes in some nice sections of rock and is a great, long outing for a sunny winter afternoon. The route begins with *Finger Traverse* and follows parts of many lines up and left across the face, finishing at the top of the Tourist Gully left of the Kissing Camels. Check the topo for the exact line. FA: Pete Croff and Bob Stauch, 1960s.

53   Finger Ramp (7) ★★ 1 pitch. This is another Garden classic. Begin at the toe of the face below an obvious ramp. Climb runout rock to the first bolt and continue up the ramp to the base of the Finger. Edge around the left side of the Finger (5.7) and belay at a chain anchor in an alcove. 4 bolts and fixed pins to a 2-drilled-eyebolt anchor. FA: Richard Borgman and Steve Cheyney, 1960.

East Face

The following routes are on the East Face of North Gateway Rock. Access them from the main visitor parking lot on the northeast corner of the formation. Walk south on the paved trail to the southeast corner of the rock. Scramble up to the cliff base. Routes are listed left to right.

54   Max's Mayhem (10a) ★ 2 pitches. This is the obvious crack system on the left side of the face. Expect good big-hand crack climbing and an off-width and chimney section on sandy rock. To access the base of the route, climb (5.5) a short wall with potholes to a ledge below the crack. **Pitch 1:** Jam and layback the right-leaning crack (5.10a and 1 fixed pin) to a small belay stance with a 2-drilled-piton anchor on the left. **Pitch 2:** Work up the awkward and sandy chimney to an off-width (5.9) to a belay in the notch above. **Descent:** Scramble onto the ledge above the Finger Face and make a 2-rope rappel to the base or downclimb the *Boucher-Twombly Route* (5.4) onto the sloping East Ledges. Carefully downclimb the ledge system back to the base of the climb. **Gear:** Large stoppers, big hexes, Friends to #4. A Big Bro or extra-large Camalot helps

North Gateway Rock—East Face.

protect the second pitch. FA: Don Doucette and Max Hinkle, 1965. FFA (Pitch 2): Jimmy Dunn, Doug Snively, and Stewart Green, 1971. FFA (Pitch 1): John Hall and Kurt Rasmussen, 1974.

55 Snuggles and Fall Crack (8+) ★★ 2 pitches. Perhaps the best crack climb in the Garden of the Gods. Begin by scrambling up easy rock (5.5) onto a sloping ledge system. Belay below the obvious corner crack. **Pitch 1** *(Snuggles):* Layback the crack in the right-facing corner (5.8) to a ledge with a 2-piton anchor. 2 drilled pitons. **Pitch 2** *(Fall Crack):* Jam the awkward crack (5.8+) to a piton anchor. Watch for loose blocks. 3 drilled pitons. **Descent:** Rappel the route. **Gear:** Medium stoppers, medium to large Friends, and slings for tie-offs. FA *(Snuggles):* Mike Dudley and Claudia Pinello, mid-1960s. FA *(Fall Crack):* Steve Cheyney, mid-1960s.

56 Boucher-Twombly Route (6) An old Garden classic that goes to the top of North Gateway Rock via the exposed south ridge. It is now illegal, however, to climb the last pitch over the top of the crumbling Kissing Camels. Begin by scrambling up the East Ledges past *Snuggles* to a flake system that goes left. **Pitch 1:** Climb left across the big flakes (5.5) and scramble into a gully above the Finger Face. **Pitch 2:** Climb an easy ramp system on the west side of the ridge to a belay in a notch. **Descent:** Locate rappel anchors atop Finger Face routes and rappel west with double ropes into the Tourist Gully. FA: Stan Boucher and Vernon Twombly, 1945.

57 Spam Man (9) 2 pitches. Just another funky Garden route. The first ascent party used a car jack in one of the large potholes for protection. **Pitch 1:** Climb soft sandstone through potholes (5.9) and past old pitons to a belay stance below a right-leaning crack. **Pitch 2:** Stem and climb the crack system to a belay on the East Ledges. **Descent:** Scramble south down the East Ledges. **Gear:** Some large Tri-cams are useful, and maybe a hydraulic jack too. FA: Leonard Coyne and Stewart Green, 1980.

CHAPTER TWO

South Gateway Rock

South Gateway Rock is an immense and beautiful 250-foot-high formation composed of Lyons Sandstone. The crag offers many quality routes that should not be missed by the visiting or resident rock climber. The northeast face is the home of several classic slab climbs. The steeper and sunny west face is also a worthwhile stop for any sandstone addict.

Park at the main Garden parking area at the northeast corner of North Gateway Rock. Follow the paved trail south from the lot to the Gateway gap between North and South Gateway Rocks. The Drug Wall is on the northeast side of the formation. Reach it via a couple of climber paths through the scrub oaks. To reach the west face, continue on the paved trail through the Gateway until you're west of the face. Route descriptions begin with the Drug Wall and go counterclockwise.

Drug Wall

The Drug Wall offers quality slab climbing on good, solid rock with generally excellent protection. The northeast-facing wall tends to be cool in the summer, making it a perfect climbing spot on hot days. In the winter, it tends to hold snow and ice and is colder than other Garden crags. A deep gully marks the left side of the face. Routes are described left to right from the gully on the east side of the wall.

1   **Rhineskeller (8)** 1 pitch. The climb ascends a detached pillar (Rhineskeller Tower) just left of the gully that separates Rhineskeller Tower from main South Gateway Rock. **Gear:** Stoppers, hexes, and runners for pothole threads. FA: Bob Stauch and Harvey Carter, 1960s.

2   **Candyman (10d)** ★ 1 pitch. This short, pumpy pitch starts up in the deep gully left of the main Drug Wall. It's often sandy. 3 drilled pitons to 2-piton anchor. 45'. FA: Mike Johnson, 1988.

Pete Takeda climbing Kor's Korner (5.12a), South Gateway Rock. STEWART M. GREEN PHOTO

South Gateway Rock—Drug Wall.

3   The Deal (11d) ★ 1 pitch. Start 10' right of *Candyman*. A sequential, pumpy route. 4 drilled pitons to 2-piton anchor (same as *Candyman*). FA: Eric Johnson, 1989.

4   Cocaine (10d) ★★★ 2 pitches. A classic slab route with great climbing on excellent sandstone. Most parties do only the first pitch and then rappel or downclimb a steep descent groove. Begin at the base of the slab right of the deep gully. **Pitch 1:** Follow a seam up left to a tricky traverse (5.8) left and up to a small stance. Friction right into a shallow, right-facing corner (5.10d) and smear up to anchors on an airy ledge. 6 drilled pitons to 2-piton anchor. Use runners to avoid rope drag. *Ninety-nine Percent Pure* (5.11d), a direct variation, avoids the left traverse. Tenuous friction leads straight up to the short corner. **Pitch 2:** Climb directly above the belay through an open corner (5.9+). Continue up and left through potholes to a belay in an obvious notch. 4 drilled pitons. **Descent:** From the top of pitch 1, rappel with 2 ropes or downclimb a shallow gully (5.4). From the top of pitch 2, downclimb south from the notch. FA: Leonard Coyne, Ken Sims, and Ed Webster, 1977.

5   Cold Turkey (11b/c R) ★★ 1 pitch. Has cold turkey got you on the run? It's the title of a popular song by John Lennon from the early seventies. After the third bolt on *Cocaine,* go left up a high-angle slab (5.11b/c) to a final runout to a belay on a narrow ledge. This pitch has great slab climbing on solid rock. 9 drilled pitons. Descend down the gully or rappel from *Cocaine's* anchors. FA: Bob D'Antonio and Richard Aschert, 1984.

6   Stalagmite (8) 1 pitch. This seldom-climbed route starts from the top of *Cold Turkey* and climbs up a shallow, right-facing corner past 5 fixed pins. Loose and probably not worth the effort. **Gear:** Medium nuts. FA: Richard Borgman, 1960s. FFA: Dick Long, 1960s.

7   Silver Spoon (5) ★★ 1 pitch. An excellent beginner climb up the lower Drug Wall slab. Start is the same as *Cocaine*. Climb straight up to the first bolt. Follow a seam up left to the left side of the big roof. Traverse right under the roof to a 2-piton belay in a gully. 2 bolts and 2 fixed pitons. **Descent:** Rappel or downclimb the gully. FA: Stewart Green, Steve Westbay, and Kurt Rasmussen, 1972.

8   There Goes the Neighborhood (10c) ★ 1 pitch. Wow! A roof climb in the Garden. Start the same as *Silver Spoon* and climb up to the fourth fixed pin. Pull up left out the big roof. Finish up a slab to the *Cocaine* belay. FA: Peter Gallagher and Bryan Becker, 1981.

9   Tudor (8 R) ★ 1 pitch. A nice slab pitch that starts just right of *Silver Spoon* and climbs past 2 fixed pins to the *Silver Spoon* belay. FA: Larry Shubarth and Greg Stevens, 1981.

10   The Fixer (10a) ★★ 2 pitches. Good slab climbing up some clean rock just right of a gully. Rap off after the first pitch as the second is loose and not worth the effort. Some of the fixed pitons need replacing. Use caution. Start just right of the chopped steps on the descent gully. **Pitch 1:** Smear up the steep slab along a line of fixed pins. The crux is at the fourth bolt. It can be climbed straight up (5.11a) or to the left (5.10a). After the last piton, climb easy but runout rock (5.5) for 50' to a large pothole with anchors. Most parties rappel from the pothole after the first pitch. **Pitch 2:** Climb up a short, steep crack with gear to the top. FA (Pitch 1): Ed Webster and Leonard Coyne, 1977. FA (Pitch 2): Stewart Green and Steve McCartt, 1972.

11   Pure Energy (11c) ★★ 1 pitch. Good energy and some impeccable slab climbing technique will get you to the anchor. This wonderful slab route starts just right of *The Fixer.* Follow a line of 6 fixed pitons up a steep wall. The delicate, smearing crux is between the second and third bolts. Trust those feet! **Descent:** Rappel 100' with double ropes from a 3-bolt anchor. FA: Kerry Gunther, 1991.

12   Rocket Fuel (11b) ★★★ This is one of the area's best slab routes and was a major breakthrough in Garden friction climbing. This classic pitch frictions up a steep slab left of *Mighty Thor.* The route has 2 distinct cruxes, one at the third bolt and again at the eighth bolt just before the belay ledge. 7 fixed pitons. **Descent:** Rappel 100' with double ropes from a 3-bolt anchor to the ground. FA: Mark Rolofson and Bob D'Antonio, 1983.

13   Mighty Thor (10b) ★★ 1 pitch. This well-protected line stems and pulls up a water groove just right of *Rocket Fuel.* The crux is harder for short climbers. **Descent:** Rappel 100' with double ropes from a 3-bolt anchor to the ground. **Gear:** Bring 14 quickdraws. FA: Mark Rolofson, Bob Robertson, Murray Judge, and Gugi Rylegis, 1979.

14   ·Crescent Corner (9+) ★ 1 pitch. This is a popular and pumpy climb to the first set of anchors. The original route followed the crescent crack to *Mighty Thor's* belay, but the upper section is runout and grungy. Begin right of *Mighty Thor* below the obvious crescent crack. Pull over a series of overlaps to a lower-off anchor. 4 fixed pitons to a 2-piton anchor. FFA: Don Peterson and Helmut Husman, 1972.

15   Southeast Ridge of Block Tower (9) ★ A good pitch with a complex approach. Scramble up the Practice Slab on the west side of South Gateway Rock to the south side of Block Tower, the semidetached pinnacle that hangs above the skyline notch on the north side of the formation. Scramble up a short gully on the south side of the tower to the base of the route. Climb up past 2 fixed pins to a 2-pin anchor. **Descent:** Rappel 85' to the top of the Practice Slab. FA: Steve "Muff" Cheyney and Pete Croft, 1960s. FFA: Earl Wiggins and Cheryl Wiggins, 1975.

West Face

The west face of South Gateway Rock offers some excellent one- to three-pitch routes with a sunny western exposure that is perfect for winter afternoon cragging and early morning climbing in summer. The sandstone is generally not as solid as the Drug Wall and most of the routes have some runout sections. Routes are described left to right from the northwest corner of the formation.

16   Staircase (8 R) ★ A 4-pitch route that ascends the left edge of the Practice Slab and continues up the formation's upper north ridge to the summit. The upper pitch is rarely climbed and probably for good reasons. The first couple pitches are the best. Start at the northwest corner of South Gateway below a crack and hanging block. **Pitch 1:** Climb the crack (5.7) to a belay atop the block. **Pitch 2:** Edge up an unprotected slab to a piton belay in the obvious skyline notch, or climb the left edge of the Practice Slab. **Pitch 3:** Traverse across an exposed ledge system on the east side of Block Tower and scramble into a gully. **Pitch 4:** Work up the mostly unprotected north ridge to the rock's summit. **Descent:** Downclimb (5.5) west into a gully or scramble south down the ridge to a 2-piton anchor. **Gear:** Large stoppers, small to medium Friends, and hexes. FA: Steve Cheyney, Bob Stauch, and Pete Croff, 1964.

17   Insignificant, But There (10) 1 pitch. Boulder problem or toprope. A one-move wonder that leads up to the base of the Practice Slab. FA: Mike Johnson and Bob D'Antonio, 1983.

18   Practice Slab (1–8 TR) ★ A great beginner's toprope area with lots of variations—take your pick. Scramble up to the base of the obvious, smooth, west-facing slab. Access the toprope anchors atop the slab by climbing some chopped steps for 40' on the right side of the slab or by climbing a short headwall with chopped steps on the far right and walking north along a narrow ledge. FA: Unknown.

19   Notch Traverse (5 R) 1 pitch. A short, traversing pitch that was once very popular. Begin from the top of the Practice Slab and follow the line of least resistance up left across a slab to a 2-piton belay on the exposed notch on the northern skyline. **Descent:** Make an airy 2-rope, mostly free rappel off the Notch.

20   Tower Crack (10) A toprope! What more can you say. Watch for general looseness. FA: Toproped by Bob Robertson, 1982.

21   Sandman (7) If you like dirty and sandy chimney climbing, then this route is for you! **Gear:** Large nuts and Friends. FA: Harvey Carter, 1960s.

22   Kor's Korner (12-) ★★ 2 pitches. A classic route for the grade. Leonard Coyne made a great effort to free climb this beautiful route, one of the first 5.12s in the Garden of the Gods. Start right of the Practice Slab below an obvious semidetached pillar split by a thin crack system. **Pitch 1:** Scramble up to the left

South Gateway Rock—West Face

side of the pillar and traverse right and around a blunt arête to gain the crack. Jam the finger crack (5.12) to a 2-piton hanging belay. Most climbers rap from here. 7 fixed pitons. **Pitch 2:** Follow a line of 5 drilled pitons to a rightward traverse (5.11a) and finish up past another fixed pin to the top of the pillar. **Descent:** Make a 2-rope rappel off the backside. The anchors need replacing! **Gear:** Many small stoppers, TCUs, Friends to #2, and quickdraws. FA: Layton Kor and Gary Zielger, 1960s. FFA (Pitch 1): Leonard Coyne, 1979. FFA (Pitch 2): Richard Aschert, 1985.

23   West Point Crack (7+) ★★ 3 pitches. Very popular and a great outing. **Pitch 1:** Start 75' right of *Kor's Korner* at the left side of a large cave/pothole. Climb up a steep face past 3 fixed pins to a good belay ledge with a piton and a railroad spike for anchors. **Pitch 2:** Edge straight up (5.7) past 2 fixed pins and jam your carcass into the wide chimney. Stem up the chimney to a piton belay atop the pillar to the left. **Pitch 3:** Step south from the pillar to the main wall and climb past 2 fixed pins and some gear placements to the top. **Descent:** Scramble down gullies to the south or rappel from poor anchors atop the pillar. **Gear:** Medium to large Friends, Tri-cams, slings, and quickdraws. FA: U.S. Army climbers, 1940s. FFA: Harvey Carter, 1950s.

24   Pipe Route (10d) ★★ 2 pitches. An excellent and exposed route that should be more popular now than it is. The name came after the first ascent party used a big pipe wedged in a pothole for protection. Watch for route-finding difficulties on the first pitch. Earl Wiggins rebolted the line with modern bolts in 1998 to make a safer climb. **Pitch 1:** Begin on the right side of a small cave. Pull up potholes past some bolts until it's possible to trend up right to a 2-bolt belay atop a flake. **Pitch 2:** Follow a line of bolts up the steep white wall to a 2-bolt belay/rappel anchor on a ledge between flakes. A rotten third pitch climbs up right past an old fixed piton to the top. **Descent:** Rappel the route from the top of pitch 2 with 2 ropes or with a single 60-meter rope. **Gear:** Medium nuts, slings, and quickdraws. FA: John Auld and Gary Ziegler, 1960s. FFA: Earl Wiggins and Jim Souder, 1976.

25   Indian Head (9+ R) 2 pitches. Rarely climbed route up potholes between the white and red sandstone profile of an Indian head. Climb the first 45' of the *Pipe Route* to 2 pins at the base of a shallow left-facing corner (the Indian head profile). Make a hard move past the pins, and then follow the corner up to a belay ledge. Loose climbing up the profile of the Indian head leads to a belay ledge and safety. **Gear:** Many stoppers, nuts, and Friends to #3. FA: Steve Hong, Ed Webster, and Earl Wiggins, 1976.

26   Pipe Dreams (10d R) ★★ 3 pitches. More like a nightmare for the unprepared! This route is a soft sandstone classic and a must-do for climbers competent at the grade. Start below a flake/crack system left of the Tombstone wafer pinnacle. **Pitch 1:** Swing up the flake crack (watch out—it's falling apart!) and continue up past 4 fixed pins (5.10). Make a right traverse past a couple

South Gateway Rock—West Face.

more pins to a 2-piton belay. **Pitch 2:** Work up left through some potholes with marginal protection to a huge pothole. Pull past and climb the headwall (5.9) above past 2 pitons to a belay stance. **Pitch 3:** Face climb up rotten rock past 1 manky fixed piton to the top. **Gear:** Medium to large nuts and Friends. FA: Earl Wiggins, Ed Webster, and Steve Hong, 1976.

27   Credibility Gap (9+) ★★★ 2 pitches. The second pitch is rarely climbed. This route is another must-do line for the visiting climber. Great protection, beautiful moves, and good exposure all add up to one of the best routes in the Garden of the Gods. Start behind the Tombstone block. **Pitch 1:** Grab potholes and edges (5.9+) up the line between the white and red sandstone. Watch for occasional loose holds and the long runout to the first pin. 7 fixed pitons to a 2-eyebolt lowering anchor, 75'. **Pitch 2:** Climb up left (5.8) past a couple of old pins to a short 5.6 corner. Climb the corner and then the face above to the top of the wall. FA: Gary Zielger and John Auld, 1960s. FFA: Morgan Gadd and Skip Hamilton, 1970.

28   Dog Day Afternoon (11a) 2 pitches. An excellent, well-protected route that is seldom climbed. **Pitch 1:** Climb *Credibility Gap* to its belay anchors. **Pitch 2:** Make an airy traverse (5.10d) up right on loose flakes and potholes to the ridge. 8 drilled pitons. FA: Mark Rolofson and Ed Webster, 1978.

NOTE: Some superb high boulder problems are found right of *Credibility Gap* and just left of the chopped steps leading up to a shallow amphitheater. A drilled piton anchor in a pothole can be used for toprope protection on *Sewing Machine* (B1 FA: Earl Wiggins, 1975), a high bouldering test piece. Just right of *Sewing Machine* are *High Step* and *Smear Test* (FA both: Stewart Green, 1972). Both are desperate B1+ slab problems.

29   South End Tower—North Arête (9+) A short route up the north side of a pillar right of some slabs. Climb an easy corner and belay on a ledge. Step right and climb the prow past a single fixed pin. FA: Harvey Carter, 1982.

30   South End Tower—West Face (10b) 1 pitch. A good, short route on good rock. Climb out of the corner and edge up the face past a pin to a pothole and a final pin that protects the crux. **Gear:** A #6 Hexentric or a Tri-cam works well in a pothole. FA: Harvey Carter, 1982.

31   Southwest Crack (9) 1 pitch. A crack and corner system on the outside face of a pillar. Maybe it's better to toprope it. **Gear:** Medium nuts and quickdraws. FA: Ed Webster and Harvey Carter, 1982.

32   The Renegade (11a/b) 1 pitch. A good, pumpy route hidden in the upper canyon below the summit of South Gateway Rock. Access by scrambling north up a gully into the canyon. Look for pins along a right-angling seam on the right-hand (west-facing) wall. Face climb up the seam to a pothole. Make a thin move out of the hole to a 2-piton anchor on ridge above. 4 drilled pitons. **Descent:** Rappel 55'. FA: Ian Spencer-Green and Stewart Green, 1993.

CHAPTER THREE

Red and White Twin Spires

Red Twin Spire

Red Twin Spire, a 60-foot-high pinnacle comprised of soft Lyons Sandstone, sits in the middle of the Gateway between North and South Gateway Rocks. Four routes ascend to the summit of Red Twin Spire. The classic and well-protected *Potholes,* on the northeast side, is the most popular climb. Red Twin and its smaller neighbor White Twin Spire are encircled by a paved sidewalk, making it a popular spot for tourists to watch rock climbers at play. Routes are described from right to left when facing the spire from the east.

1   **North Ridge (9)** A toprope up the north face and ridge. FA: Unknown.

2   **Potholes (7)** ★★ A classic face climb through a series of potholes on the northeast side of the tower. 4 fixed pitons to 2-piton belay/rappel anchor on the summit. FA: Mike Borgoff, 1950s.

3   **Incline Ledge (8 R)** Best to toprope this one. Start left of *Potholes* and take a course up a sloping ramp to a small overhang, then straight up to the summit anchors. 2 fixed pitons. FA: Harvey Carter, 1950s.

4   **South Ridge (9 R)** Classic but runout. The route takes a direct line up the south ridge. The crux, a hard move over a small overhang, is encountered in the first 20' of climbing. 2 fixed pitons. FA: Unknown, 1960s.

White Twin Spire

This beautiful, 55-foot-high spire, composed of white Fountain Sandstone, offers several classic and popular routes on solid rock. White Twin is the western neighbor of higher Red Twin Spire. Several popular classics ascend the spire, including the *South Ridge,* one of the most climbed Garden routes. The west face routes are usually toproped.

Descent: Descent off all routes is by rappelling 55' west from a 2-piton anchor with chains on the tiny summit.

Red Twin Spire.

White Twin Spire.

1   North Ridge (7 R) ★★
An exciting line up the right side of the narrow ridge on solid rock. 2 fixed pitons. **Gear:** Medium stoppers, hexes, or Friends, and quickdraws. FA: Paul Radigen, 1950s. FFA: Harvey Carter, late 1950s.

2   North Ridge Eliminate (10 TR) ★★ Save your body parts and toprope this unprotected route up the flat face of the north ridge. FA: Don Petersen, 1972.

3   West Face (8) ★★★
Often toproped. A classic, short face climb up the sunny west face of White Spire. Several variations are possible. Begin on the left side of the face. Climb past an undercling, and hand traverse right along a flake system to the right side of the face. Move up and then swing left onto a two-hand

Ed Webster raps off Red Twin Spire. STEWART M. GREEN PHOTO

pothole edge and finish straight up. 3 fixed pitons. FA: Harvey Carter and Art Howells, 1963.

4   Kor Route (10a R) ★★ A right-hand start to the *West Face*. Ascend a steep face (5.10a) up to a flake ledge. Continue up the upper section of the *West Face* to the summit. FA: Layton Kor, 1964.

5   Mantle Route (11-) ★★ This route is a short, hard variation up the left edge of the west face. Begin from the flake ledge and mantle up left on a series of rounded bumps to the north ridge. FA: Steve Cheyney, 1971.

6   South Ridge (6) ★★★ A classic, moderate romp up the solid, south ridge of the spire. Start at the base of the narrow south ridge. Climb cracks and edges to the summit. 2 fixed pitons. **Gear:** Medium stoppers and hexes. FA: Harvey Carter, 1957.

CHAPTER FOUR

Grey Rock (aka Kindergarten Rock)

Grey Rock, also called Kindergarten Rock, is a large, imposing formation in the south section of the Garden of the Gods. The rock, composed of Upper Lyons Sandstone, offers many excellent routes that feature sharp, in-cut edges on compact rock. The formation has two distinct summits. The south summit routes are some of the finest and the most popular lines in the Garden of the Gods. The north summit routes are not as popular and the rock is often of dubious quality with many removable handholds. Most of the routes are protected by bolts or drilled pitons. Grey Rock also has some classic crack routes that require natural gear to protect them. There is also excellent bouldering at the Snake Pit Boulders east of the road on the southeast side of Grey Rock.

All the former parking areas along the park road below the east face of the formation are now closed. Park at a pullout at the top of the hill south of Grey Rock or at a large paved parking area just south of the hill. Hike down the road and then follow climber trails to the base of the east face. Reach the west face by following a trail up a canyon south and west of the cliff. Alternatively you can park at the main visitor lot on the northeast flank of North Gateway Rock and follow trails and roads south to Grey Rock. Routes on the east face are described left to right.

East Face South Summit

1   **Antline Direct (10 R)** ★ 2 pitches. Seldom ascended. Loose climbing on somewhat dubious holds makes an exciting outing. Thin face moves on soft rock lead past a fixed pin to the obvious crack system. Start on the far left side (south) of the east face. **Pitch 1:** Face climb up a thin, loose face to a drilled piton. Continue straight up past a small tree to a belay atop a pillar. **Pitch 2:**

Heidi Knapp laments the End of an Era (5.8), Grey Rock STEWART M. GREEN PHOTO

Grey Rock—East Face.

Work up an obvious crack that ranges from fingers to wide hands. End on ledges on the broad South Ridge. **Descent:** Go left on the South Ridge and downclimb easy slabs. **Gear:** Medium to large nuts and Friends. FA: Unknown, 1960s. FFA: Bob D'Antonio and Larry Kledzik, 1981.

2   Skyline Pig (10b R) ★★ 2 pitches. Excellent face climbing up a steep face to a finishing corner. The route has been rebolted to make it safer. **Pitch 1:** Start 100' up right of *Antline Direct.* Climb a short, unprotected face to the first pin and safety. Continue straight up past more fixed pitons and bolts and then step left to a belay ledge with a 2-cold-shut anchor. **Pitch 2:** Move up right and stem up a right-facing corner with 3 cold shuts to a 2-cold-shut anchor. **Descent:** Downclimb easy slabs on the South Ridge or rappel the route. **Gear:** Quickdraws. FA: Don Doucette and friends, 1972. FFA: Steve Hong and Steve Gropp, 1976.

3   Anarchy (12a) ★★ 1 pitch. One of the hardest sport routes in the Garden. Thin edge climbing with 2 distinct cruxes. Step up left to begin. Follow bolts for 70'. 7 bolts to 2-bolt anchor. FA: Ric Geiman, 1991.

4   Beat Me Up Scotty (10d) ★★ 1 pitch. Sounds like a personal problem. Excellent climbing on solid flakes and sharp edges. 7 drilled pitons to 2-piton anchor. FA: Mike Johnson, 1991.

5   Black and Blue (8+ R) 2 pitches. What your body will look like if you fall getting to the first piton! Good climbing but bad fixed gear and long runouts make this unpopular. **Gear:** Medium stoppers and Friends. FA: Pete Croff and Steve Cheyney, 1965.

6   The Extremist (12a) ★★ 1 pitch. Thin moves past the second bolt lead to easier climbing. The second clip is tough—don't blow it! Better yet, stick-clip it. 6 bolts to 2-bolt anchor. FA: Ric Geiman and Ed Schmidt, 1991.

7   Alligator Soup (11d) ★★ 2 pitches. Great climbing. This route is much safer since it was retrobolted. Most parties just do the excellent first pitch (5.10a). The second pitch is 5.11d. Watch your rope so it doesn't get sliced on any sharp flakes. **Pitch 1:** Start off a boulder and climb a sloping ramp 10' left of *Diesel and Dust.* Swing past 3 fixed pins to the crux—going left of the pins is 5.10a, going right of the pins is 5.11a. Continue straight up past 5 fixed pitons to a belay anchor at a small ledge. 8 bolts to 2-bolt anchor. 70'. **Pitch 2:** Face climb straight up to a small overhang with a hard move at the third pin. Crank the crux and pull several hard sections to a 2-bolt belay anchor. 9 bolts to 2-bolt anchor. **Descent:** Make 2 rappels with a single rope or a 165' rappel with double ropes from the top anchors. FA (Pitch 1): Leonard Coyne and Ed Russell, 1977. FA (Pitch 2): Ric Geiman and Cindy Geiman, 1992.

8   Margaritaville (8 R/X) 1 pitch. A scary and dangerous climb. Better to toprope it from nearby anchors. The route starts on a flake just right of *Alligator Soup.* Watch for some loose stuff. FA: Ed Webster and Mack Johnson, 1977.

Grey Rock—East Face.

9   Diesel and Dust (11a) ★★ 2 pitches. Another excellent and popular sport line. Most parties just do the first pitch. **Pitch 1:** Climb a steep face 10' left of *New Era*. Follow a line of 7 bolts (5.11a crux at fifth bolt) to a belay ledge with anchors. 7 bolts to 2-bolt anchor. 75'. **Pitch 2:** Traverse left and crank past 7 bolts up a steep face to belay anchors. 7 bolts to 2-bolt anchor. **Descent:** Rappel the route after the second pitch. With double ropes you can rappel 165' to the ground. FA: Ric Geiman and Cindy Geiman, 1990.

10   New Era (7) ★★★ 3 pitches. This megaclassic route is pretty hard to miss. Follow the large dihedral for 3 pitches to the top. Many parties rappel from the top of pitch 2 to avoid the walk-off. The crux is an exposed layback on pitch 2. **Pitch 1:** Face climb easy rock to the corner and belay on a stance with 2 drilled pitons. **Pitch 2:** Layback, jam, and face climb up the spectacular open book (5.7) to a 2-piton belay niche. **Pitch 3:** Climb left out of the niche and face climb to the ridge above. Belay wherever it's comfortable. **Descent:** Make a double-rope rappel 165' from the second belay. From the top of the route, scramble down the South Ridge from the summit. **Gear:** Large stoppers, Friends to #3.5, and quickdraws. FA: Harvey Carter and friends, 1959.

11   New Generation (10c) ★★★ 2 pitches. A great route on good rock with excellent protection and superb position. **Pitch 1:** Climb the first pitch of *Diesel and Dust* to its 2-bolt belay stance. **Pitch 2:** Work up right and follow a line of bolts up edges on a steep face to a belay stance. 4 fixed pitons to 2-piton anchor. **Gear:** Some Tri-cams and Friends might be useful in pockets. **Descent:** Traverse off left or rappel route. FA: Current line by Mike Johnson in 1989 but previously climbed with scant pro by Earl Wiggins in the 1970s.

12   Binary (11a) ★ 1 pitch. This long pitch climbs the first 15' of *New Era* before breaking right on a vertical face. Follow a line of homemade red hangers to high anchors. 8 bolts to 2-bolt anchor. **Gear:** Medium gear for the start and quickdraws for the bolts. FA: Bob Robertson and Carrie Robertson, 1991.

13   Death of the Dinosaur (10a) ★★ 1 pitch. This is a direct start to the *End of an Era* arête. Begin left of the arête. Crank past a bolt (5.10a) and continue up a line of bolts along the left side of the sharp arête. FA: Bryan Becker and Ric Geiman, 1991.

14   End of an Era (8+) ★★★ Classic. Aesthetic face climbing up the sharp arête right of *New Era*. Several variations are possible. Step around the corner from the first pin or climb directly up the right side of the arête before reaching left to a jug. 5 fixed pitons to 2-piton anchor. 75'. **Gear:** Medium cams for the start. FA: George Allen and Ann Liebold, 1979.

15   End to End (10a) ★★ 1 pitch. Excellent, overhanging, and pumpy face climbing on the right side of the arête. 6 drilled pitons to 2-piton anchor (same as *End of an Era*). FA: Mike Johnson and Lou Kalina, 1986.

16   Bob's Buttress Crack (8+) ★★ 2 pitches. More face than crack climbing. Excellent, although a bit dirty. Most climbers just do the first pitch. Climb the obvious crack system to a 2-piton belay below a wide crack. 60'. **Gear:** Large stoppers and Friends to #3. FA: Don Doucette and Mike Dudley, 1965. FFA: Jim Dunn and Stewart Green, 1971, but toproped free previously.

17   Sandy Monster (9+) ★★ A face route that is often sandy after rain. Follow a line of bolts just right of *Bob's Buttress* and left of deep *Ormes Chimney.* 4 fixed pitons to 2-piton anchor. FA: Dan Durland, 1991.

18   Ormes Chimney (6) Best to leave this to the pigeons. A dirty chimney route. FA: The great Colorado climbing pioneer Robert Ormes in 1925.

East Face North Summit

Most of the routes on this section of Grey Rock are loose, dangerous, and not much fun. The rock is soft and friable, making the protection dubious at best. Use extreme caution when climbing in this area and wear a helmet. Come prepared for both an adventure and an epic.

19   Hong-Fiedler Route (8 R/X) 1 pitch. This route is not worth dying on. Climb a short corner past 4 drilled pins, traverse up and right to a short corner (5.7) with no gear. Run it out to the top (5.7 X). FA: Steve Hong and Carol Fiedler, 1977.

Grey Rock—East Face North Summit.

20   Big Sky (7) ★★ 1 pitch. Popular and fun. This short pitch is a retrobolted version of the start of the *Hong-Fiedler Route*. Climb a corner with 4 drilled pitons to a 2-piton anchor. FA: Tom Geiman and Ric Geiman, 1992.

21   Five-Eight Crack (8) Approach this and the next route from the summit saddle via a third-class ledge. Jam and face climb the obvious crack. **Gear:** Medium to large nuts and Friends. FA: Unknown.

22   Gronk (10) A hand crack on soft rock. Wow, what a treat! Traverse across a ledge to the righthand crack system. **Gear:** Medium to large nuts and Friends. FA: Bryan Becker and Ed Webster, 1977.

23   Bilbo's Bag Ends (10a R) 3 pitches. Watch out on this sandy nightmare. A long route up loose white rock on the right side of the north summit wall. **Gear:** Medium to large nuts and Friends. FA: Ed Webster and Bryan Becker, 1977.

24   North Ridge (4 R) Classic but hard to protect. Climb a corner just left of the north ridge. After 75' traverse right (5.4 R) onto the north ridge proper. Waltz up the ridge to the airy north summit. FA: Robert Ormes, 1926.

25   North Ridge Direct (8 R) Climb directly up the north ridge from the base of the prow with no protection. Continue up the *North Ridge* to the summit. FA: Stanley Boucher and Vernon Twombly, 1946.

West Face

Grey Rock's west face is divided into two walls. The wall below the north summit is broken and rotten. The wall below the south summit offers a selection of excellent routes on generally good flakes. Be extremely careful that your rope doesn't get sliced by any flakes. One fatality occurred in 1993 when a climber fell and his rope was cut. It's a good idea to use double ropes on some of the routes.

Approach the west face by hiking up to the gap between Grey Rock and Keyhole Rock. Follow a climber's path southwest to the base of the obvious face. Routes are described left to right.

26   Frankenstein (8 R) 2 pitches. Loose and runout. This route is not the safest in the Garden. Watch for flexible flakes. **Pitch 1:** Edge up the face left of the obvious left-facing corner past 4 fixed pins to a ledge belay. **Pitch 2:** Finish up easier rock (5.5) to the ridge. **Gear:** Medium nuts, Friends, and long slings for tying off chickenheads. FA: Ken Sims and Leonard Coyne, 1977.

27   Monster Crack (8) ★★ 1 pitch. Excellent laybacking and wide crack climbing. Jam and layback up the narrow left-facing corner system. It's possible to belay in the wide middle section. The upper crack is the crux. Layback or jam it. 1 fixed piton to 2-piton anchor. An upper pitch follows fourth-class rock up and left to the summit ridge. **Gear:** Large stoppers and medium to large Friends. FA: Harvey Carter and Paul Radigen, 1950s.

Grey Rock—West Face.

28   Scarecrow (10b R) ★★ 1 pitch. Thin hand and finger crack-climbing. The rock has cleaned up nicely with traffic. Begin by climbing up left along a narrow ramp system to the base of the crack. Jam the steep crack (5.10) to a ledge with a 2-piton anchor. **Descent:** Rappel 125' with double ropes. **Gear:** Large stoppers and Friends to #3. FA: Harvey Carter and Gary Ziegler, 1967. FFA: Jim Dunn and Stewart Green, 1973.

29   Lance (6) 2 pitches. Not too bad of an effort for a route done in the 1920s. Climb the chimney and ramp system up left to the ridge north of the south summit. FA: Albert Ellingwood and friends, 1925.

30   Sword in the Stone (8) ★ 1 pitch. A contrived but fun route. Begin off the ledge right of *Lance*. Edge up the steep slab (5.8) and, at the third pin, begin traversing up left (5.7) past 3 more pitons to *Lance's* chimney. Finish up *Lance*. **Gear:** Slings for tie-offs. FA: Ed Webster and Leonard Coyne, 1976.

31   Footloose and Fancy Free (11a) ★★★ 1 pitch. A classic route that is a must-do—make every effort to climb *Footloose*. Use lots of runners and double ropes to avoid cutting your rope on sharp flakes. Start by climbing a fun slab with 5 pitons to the base of a steep, left-facing corner. Edge up the corner and make airy moves over a roof that caps the corner. Crank perfect edges to a belay ledge. 14 fixed pitons to 2-piton anchor. **Descent:** Scramble down ledges and gullies south. Don't rappel—the edges are too sharp. **Gear:** Medium stoppers, Friends #2.5 and #3, and quickdraws. FA: Leonard Coyne and Ed Webster, 1977.

32   Fragile Dihedral (12- TR) Toprope. Flexible holds and hard moves up a right-facing dihedral. FA: Bob D'Antonio, 1985.

33   South End Slabs (2–8 TR) A good beginner's area. Set up a toprope from 2 sets of double eyebolts and have some fun. FA: Unknown.

CHAPTER FIVE

Keyhole Rock

This excellent formation offers a number of great, short routes. With both eastern and western exposures, the climber can play hide and seek with the sun depending on the season. Many small ledges are situated conveniently along the cliffs, allowing easy access to the climbs. All of the routes described are one pitch long unless otherwise noted. Descent off most of the routes is by walking off on ledges or rappelling from fixed anchors. Toprope anchors are sometimes difficult to set up for many of these routes. Use trees with caution as most pine trees have shallow root systems.

The best access to Keyhole Rock is from two conveniently located parking areas on Juniper Way Loop. For climbs at the northern end of Keyhole Rock, park at a large parking area at the intersection of Juniper Way Loop and Garden Drive. For the southern area and east face of Keyhole Rock, park at the south parking lot on Juniper Way Loop.

East Face First Tier—South End

1   **Dancin' Fool (10a)** ★★ Good face climbing on excellent rock. Start at the south end of the east face of Keyhole Rock on the lower tier. 5 drilled pitons to tree anchor. **Descent:** Walk off. FA: Peter Gallagher and Larry Shubarth, 1980.

2   **Breeze Crack (6)** Not such a breeze if you can't place natural gear. The obvious line right of the cave formation. Watch for loose rock. **Gear:** Medium stoppers, hexes, and Friends. FA: Unknown.

3   **True Grit (8 R)** ★ Although it's runout in some places, this route is still worth doing. 4 drilled pitons. FA: Pete Croft, Leonard Coyne, and Mark Rolofson, 1976.

4   **Brand-X Caper (10+ R/X)** Best to toprope this one. There is a long runout getting to the crux that keeps most climbers at bay. This dangerous climb has both loose holds and long runouts, and has been the site of a fatality. Face climb up a steep wall past several potholes. Watch out for bad pro. 3 drilled pitons. FA: Ed Webster, Leonard Coyne, Steve Johnson, and Mark Rolofson, 1977.

Keyhole Rock East Face, First Tier—South End.

Keyhole Rock East Face—First Tier.

5   **Buttress Climb (7)** This climb is located on the far right side of the lower south tier. Follow the slabby buttress past 3 drilled pitons. FA: Harvey Carter, 1975.

South End Second Tier

A long ledge separates the second tier from the lower first tier. Access the following routes by hiking up left of *Dancin' Fool* or scrambling up a gully right of the *Buttress Climb*. Routes are described left to right from the south end of the tier.

6   **South Ridge (7 TR)** Just toprope it. A fun moderate with no protection that follows the right side of the south ridge. FA: Unknown.

7   **Martian Route (8)** ★ Good climbing with some loose holds. 4 drilled pitons. FA: Unknown Martians, 1981.

8   **The Water Gully (7)** Fun climbing but kind of runout. Edge up the obvious water groove. 2 fixed pitons. FA: Unknown.

9   **Andromeda (9)** ★★ A short, classic pitch with excellent moves on good rock. 4 drilled pitons. FA: Dennis Harmon, Bob D'Antonio, and Larry Kledzik, 1982.

10   **Etho-Babble (11c)** A short, steep face. 4 drilled pitons. FA: Mark Milligan and Brent Kertzman, 1986.

Keyhole Rock East Face—Third Tier.

11   Space Ship Orion (10a R) Climb a face above a pedestal to the ridgeline. 1 drilled piton. FA: Bob D'Antonio, Dennis Harmon, and Larry Kledzik, 1982.

12   Space Invaders (10a R) They're back! Thin, friable face-climbing. 1 drilled piton. FA: Bob D'Antonio, Dennis Harmon, and Larry Kledzik, 1982.

13   J-Crack (7 R) This route starts 200' right and down from *Space Invaders* at the base of an obvious left-angling crack. **Gear:** Medium nuts and Friends to #4. FA: Unknown.

14   Dihedral (9+ R) Start just right of a gully and 50' right of J-Crack. **Gear:** Medium stoppers. FA: Unknown.

South End Third Tier

The Third Tier is the uppermost tier on the eastside of Keyhole Rock. The south end of the tier, however, dips into a low wash at the far southern end of the formation.

15   South Ridge (8 R) 3 pitches plus some scrambling. This route follows the long south ridge of Keyhole Rock to the summit. Begin in the wash below the bulging ridge. **Pitch 1:** Climb up and over the bulges (5.8 R) past a couple old fixed pitons and belay where convenient. **Pitch 2:** Start off a good belay ledge and climb the rounded ridge (5.7) past a couple pins. Scramble up the easier

Keyhole Rock East Face

and wider ridge above and belay. Scramble up the low-angle ridge (fourth class) and belay again below the final steep ridge. **Pitch 3:** Climb up the mostly unprotected but easy ridge to the summit. **Descent:** Rappel east to a ledge. FA: Harvey Carter and friend, 1950s.

16   Macbeth (10b) ★★ A Kledzik classic! This route ascends a steep face right of the lower South Ridge. 4 drilled pitons. FA: Larry Kledzik, 1981.

17   Cheap Thrills (10)   Cheap Thrills are usually the most pleasurable. Scramble several hundred feet up a gully from *Macbeth* until you're below a smooth face with a single piton. Crank edges past the pin onto the ridge. FA: Bob D'Antonio and Larry Kledzik, 1982.

18   Solo (4 R) A short, unprotected line that leads to the upper South Ridge. FA: Unknown.

19   Potholes (8 R) A good route that climbs past several large potholes. FA: Harvey Carter, 1982.

20   Ellingwood Chimney (6) ★ Quite the impressive climb for 1920! Work up the obvious chimney to the summit of Keyhole Rock. **Descent:** Rappel from a thread to the base. **Gear:** A selection of medium to large nuts and Friends. FA: Albert Ellingwood, 1920.

21   Grovel Crack (9 R) Impressive only because someone made the effort to climb this piece of choss. Grovel up the dirty off-width crack system right of the chimney. **Gear:** A selection of medium to large nuts and Friends. FA: Unknown.

22   Upper Borderline (11b R) This route ascends a steep, north-facing step to the summit of Keyhole. Start by scrambling up easy rock to an airy belay stance below the north ridge. Pull edges past a couple fixed pitons to a 2-piton anchor. FA: Ed Webster and Bob D'Antonio, 1982.

North End First Tier—East Face

Some fine, short routes ascend this section of Keyhole Rock. The cliff gets early morning sun in the winter and evening shade in the summer. It's easy to set up topropes from the big ledge atop the tier. Watch out for failing tree anchors. Routes are described left to right from a gully. Be aware that some fixed protection may be missing or stolen from some of these routes.

23   Left Out (11) Be careful, it's a long way to the first bolt. A short, steep edging problem. 2 drilled pitons. FA: Bob D'Antonio and Gene Smith, 1986.

24   Shock It to the Top (12b/c) ★★ This route boasts one of the hardest single moves in the Garden. Sequential face climbing leads to a thin crux move near the top. 5 drilled pitons. FA: Gene Smith and Bob D'Antonio, 1986.

25   Waterchute Route (12a) ★★   A classic route that was the Garden's first 5.12. The crux is getting past the first piton. Stem and edge up the obvious water groove. Fixed protection may be missing on this route. 4 drilled pitons. FFA: Leonard Coyne and Ken Sims, 1977. After their ascent the route was chopped, leaving gaping finger pockets. In 1981 Bob D'Antonio was the first to make a free ascent after it was rebolted and the pockets filled in.

26   Patty the Pig (10d) ★★   Good slab climbing, with a long runout getting to the second bolt. 2 drilled pitons. FA: Bob D'Antonio and Ed Webster, 1982.

27   Pig Dust (11d TR)   Toprope the slab line 10' right of *Patty the Pig*. FA: Bob D'Antonio and Mark Rolofson, 1983.

28   Angel Dust (10) ★   An excellent short route that was climbed solo on the first ascent. 3 drilled pitons. FA: Mark Rolofson, 1983.

29   Rocket Dust (10)   Another short line that was free soloed on the first ascent. 2 drilled pitons. FA: Bob D'Antonio, 1983.

30   Surprise (8 R) ★   Surprisingly good. Climb a face with 1 drilled piton. FA: Unknown.

31   Prodigal Son (9-)   A short, shallow corner leads to a headwall. Go left up to a ledge and the belay. 3 drilled pitons. FA: Peter Gallagher and Larry Shurbarth, 1981.

Keyhole Rock East Face—North End, First Tier

Keyhole Rock North End—First Tier.

32   The Morning After (10d) ★★ A direct finish to *Prodigal Son.* Instead of traversing, climb straight up the headwall. 4 fixed pitons. FA: Mark Rolofson and Bob Robertson, 1980.

North End Second Tier—East Face

The Second Tier's North End is above a ledge system. Access the ledge at the north end of Keyhole Rock by scrambling south up a groove southwest of Easter Rock.

33   Hound Dog (7 R) Scramble south along the ledge to the base of a face below a crack system. Climb potholes up the face (5.7 R) and follow the crack to the ridge above. **Descent:** Scramble south along the ridge crest until it's possible to downclimb east. **Gear:** Medium nuts and Friends. FA: Unknown.

34   Finger Banger (10b) ★ The route follows a right-angling crack system. A hard crux move (5.10b) leads up to a crack and a 2-piton anchor on a stance below the ridge top. **Descent:** Rappel 65'. **Gear:** Medium stoppers and quickdraws. FA: Bob D'Antonio, 1982.

35   Status Quo (9 R) Seldom climbed. A face with a couple of fixed pitons to *Finger Banger's* anchors. FA: Bob D'Antonio and Harvey Carter, 1982.

Keyhole Rock East Face—North End, Second Tier.

36   Welcome to the Garden (10b R) ★ Pretty good route but the protection is scant. Begin at the north end of the rock below an overhang. Climb out the left side of the overhang past a fixed piton, then up the steep face above past a couple more pitons to a 3-piton anchor on the ridge. **Descent:** Scramble south or rappel. FA: Bob D'Antonio and Ed Webster, 1982.

37   Borderline Direct (10b/c) ★★★ A great line with excellent moves leading up to the north ridge. Climb up right under an overhang and crank over it to a groove that leads to a 2-piton anchor. **Gear:** Medium nuts or Friends. FFA: Bob D'Antonio, 1982.

38   Borderline (10c R) ★★ A great route that ascends the steep north ridge. Climb directly up the prow of the ridge past some old, funky bolts to a 2-piton anchor in a groove on the ridge. 3 bad bolts. **Gear:** #2 and #2.5 Friends, quickdraws. FA: Harvey Carter. FFA: Earl Wiggins, Leonard Coyne, and Mark Rolofson, 1977.

West Face

The West Face of Keyhole Rock is a huge wall broken by ledges. Few routes ascend the face because the rock tends to be rotten and loose. Routes are described from left to right from *Borderline* on the formation's north ridge.

Keyhole Rock West Face—North End.

39   Small Overhang (10 TR)   A toprope route up the steep face right of *Borderline*. FA (Toprope): Bob Robertson and Fred Aschert, 1981.

40   BFD (10) ★★ *Big F#*@ing Deal* was the original name. A great short pitch on excellent rock with good protection. Begin in a gully. Climb up left using small potholes to a crux at the third piton. Continue to anchors on the ridge. 5 drilled pitons to 2-piton anchor. FA: Bob D'Antonio and Peter Gallagher, 1981.

41   Ziggy Sanddust (10a) ★★   Another great pitch with good protection that climbs past some potholes. The finishing moves are dicey. Many parties lower off the top piton. 4 drilled pitons. FA: Bob D'Antonio, Peter Gallagher, and Larry Kledzik, 1981.

42   Punk Face (10a) ★   Start high in the gully. Climb a short corner with a single drilled piton. FA: Bob D'Antonio and Larry Kledzik, 1981.

43   Punk Lives (10a)   The pothole-riddled face right of the gully. Pull pockets past 1 drilled piton and a railroad spike. FA: Bob D'Antonio and Larry Kledzik, 1981.

44   Keyhole Route 4th Class   A tourist-trap route that clambers up to the "keyhole" arch and emerges on the top of the wall behind it. Watch for broken glass on the holds! FA: Unknown Indians.

Keyhole Rock West Face.

45   Broken Glass (10a R) This and the next route are located in a hidden amphitheater above the Keyhole. A hard move at the pin leads to the top and safety. 1 drilled piton. FA: Mark Rolofson and Bob D'Antonio, 1983.

46   The Pocket Face (10 TR) Toprope a line 10' right of *Broken Glass*. FA: Mark Rolofson and Bob D'Antonio, 1983.

47   Old Aid Bolts (10d R) Scramble 300' down and right of *Punk Lives* until you see a couple of old bolts on a short face. FA: Bob D'Antonio, 1982.

48   Mission Impossible (11b R) ★★ 4 pitches. This route ascends the west face of Keyhole Rock in 4 short pitches. The last steep pitch is the crux. It follows a line of old aid pins (5.11b) to the summit of Keyhole Rock. **Pitch 1:** Start about 100 yards down and right of the Keyhole Route. Climb a short face past 1 fixed pin then up a third-class section to a belay. **Pitch 2:** Climb a steep face past 4 fixed pins to the base of a third-class gully. **Pitch 3:** Traverse up and right past a fixed pin to a belay ledge. **Pitch 4:** Climb straight up past 4 old fixed pins (crux) to a crack and the summit of Keyhole Rock. FA: Harvey Carter. FFA: Bob D'Antonio and Peter Gallagher, 1982.

49   Tempest (10d) About 200' right of *Mission Impossible* are 2 thin-looking cracks. *Tempest* is the right-hand crack. **Gear:** Medium wired stoppers, #4 Friend, and slings for potholes. FA: Ed Webster and Mack Johnson, 1982.

CHAPTER SIX

The Towers

Montezuma's Tower

Montezuma's Tower is a spectacular, freestanding, 130-foot-high pinnacle that stands alone in the middle of the Garden. The narrow pinnacle offers one of the best moderate routes in Colorado up its exposed north ridge. Descent off the tower is by rappelling 130 feet west from a 2-bolt anchor on the summit.

1   **North Ridge (7)** ★★★ 2 pitches. Classic and highly recommended. Begin at the base of the narrow north ridge. **Pitch 1:** Climb onto the north ridge via a short crack and climb past 2 large eyebolts to a ramp. Sling a pothole thread and continue up the narrowing ridge past a fixed piton and another eyebolt to an airy belay ledge with a 2-piton anchor. **Pitch 2:** Motor up the steep ridge past another eyebolt and work up a crack to a 2-eyebolt anchor on the finlike summit. **Descent:** Make a 130'-rappel with double ropes to the ground. **Gear:** A couple medium cams are useful. FA: U.S. Army climbers, 1940s. FFA: Harvey Carter, 1950.

2   **West Face (8 R)** A traversing route across the middle of the west face that is never done except by the occasional toproper. FA: John Auld, 1960s.

3   **West Face Direct (11d TR)** Good face climbing up the steep west face of the tower. FA: Toproped by Jim Dunn, 1970s.

4   **South Ridge (8/9 R)** 2 pitches. Begin below the south ridge on the southeast side of the tower. **Pitch 1:** Easy moves to a belay stance below the steep ridge. **Pitch 2:** Follows a crack system up the left side of the south ridge. 1 fixed piton. **Gear:** Some medium stoppers and hexes are useful. FA: Harvey Carter, 1958.

5   **Ruins Crack (10 R)** This route is on the west face of the Ruins, the jumble of fins on the southwest side of Montezuma's Tower. A hard start leads to a pin and easy terrain to the top. **Gear:** Medium Friends and stoppers. FA: Some long-lost soul.

6   **East Face (6 C2)** 1 or 2 pitches. This is your route if you want to do pull-ups on old quarter-inch bolts. The first part climbs a 5.7-ish crack. The upper

Climbers on the North Ridge (5.7) of Montezuma's Tower. STEWART M. GREEN PHOTO

Montezuma Tower and The Three Graces.

section follows an obvious, overhanging ladder of manky C2 bolts. FA: Harvey Carter, 1950s.

The Three Graces

This three-fin pinnacle lies just west of Montezuma's Tower. It has a couple of good routes including the *West Face* and the *Window Route,* which is an easy way to gain the exposed summit. Descent is by rappelling east from summit anchors.

1   **The Window Route (2)** ★★★ One of the better 5.2 routes you will ever climb. The route starts on the north ridge and takes a traversing line up past the "window" to a step across a crevice to the summit. **Descent:** Rappel east from anchors. **Gear:** Some medium nuts and long slings for pothole threads. FA: Unknown.

2   **Wennis Route (11a R)** The route follows the first part of an old aid line, then angles left at a hard-to-clip piton and finishes at the ridgeline. FA: Bob D'Antonio and Mark Rolofson, 1982.

3   **West Face (11a A2)** The original route up the west face. Free climb as high as you can, then aid up old bolts (A2) to a ledge. FA: Harvey Carter and Herby Hendricks, 1964. Later climbers pushed the free climbing on it.

4   **Chimney Route (2)** Begin on the south side of the formation. Work up the obvious chimney between the summit fin and the lower middle fin. FA: Unknown.

5   **East Face (10 TR)** This toprope route follows an obvious line up the east face to the summit anchors. FA: Bob D'Antonio and Bob Robertson, 1982.

Climbers on The Three Graces. STEWART M. GREEN PHOTO

Easter Rock

Easter Rock, sitting in a saddle between Grey Rock and Keyhole Rock, offers a small and airy summit for rock climbers. The pinnacle, however, is seldom climbed and for several good reasons—the rock is sandy, the protection scarce to nonexistent, and the general quality of the routes, even by Garden standards, is below par. Descent off Easter Rock is by rappelling west 60' off a 2-bolt anchor on the summit.

1   **North Ridge (9 TR)** This pumpy route up the narrow north ridge is usually toproped since all the fixed gear was pulled out long ago. Follow a line of overhanging potholes to a single piton. Follow the slabby ridge to a 2-bolt belay/rappel anchor on the summit. FA: Unknown.

2   **West Face (6 R)** ★ The classic but unprotected route to the summit. Begin on the northwest side of the spire. Climb edges (5.5) up and right onto a large ledge. It's possible to belay from a boulder here. Crank up a series of small pockets (5.6) to a scoop. Continue onto the airy ridge above and step up left to a 2-bolt anchor on the summit. The *Northwest Variation* goes left from the north side of the ledge. Climb past a 3/8" bolt with no hanger to another 3/8" bolt on the north ridge. Mantle up right onto the summit. Rappel from summit. FA: Harvey Carter.

3   **Bulge Wall (10 TR)** Edge over a bulge on the left side of the lower west face to the big ledge. FA: Stewart Green and Dave Schultz, 1972.

4   **Middle West Face (10 R)** Climb pockets to a drilled piton, cruise the crux, and run it out to the ledge. FA: Unknown.

5   **Silhouette (8)** ★ Good climbing but runout with old fixed gear. Climb a short face just left of the south ridge up to a small notch. Follow a line of 3 pitons up the ridge to the top. FA: Harvey Carter and Rusty Baille, 1968.

Pigeon Rock

Pigeon Rock is a seldom-climbed, 45-foot-high spire that sits on a low ridge in the middle of the Garden zone west of South Gateway Rock. There is no fixed protection on any of the existing climbs and the small summit has a rappel anchor. Double check the pitons and webbing before rappelling.

1   **South Ridge (4)** ★ A short climb with big holds leads to the summit. Poor protection is found near the top of the route. **Gear:** Medium stoppers and slings. FA: Unknown.

2   **West Face (6–9)** Various short faces can be toproped on the west face. FA: Unknown.

3   **North Ridge (9)** ★ The best of the 3 routes on the rock. Climb the obvious narrow prow. FA: Unknown.

Easter Rock.

ROUTES BY GRADE INDEX

ROUTES BY NAME INDEX

Features and crags are listed in capitals.

ACCESS: It's every climber's concern

The Access Fund, a national, non-profit climbers' organization, works to keep climbing areas open and to conserve the climbing environment. Need help with closures? land acquisition? legal or land management issues? funding for trails and other projects? starting a local climbers' group? CALL US!

Climbers can help preserve access by being committed to leaving the environment in its natural state. Here are some simple guidelines:

• **STRIVE FOR ZERO IMPACT** especially in environmentally sensitive areas like caves. Chalk can be a significant impact on dark and porous rock—don't use it around historic rock art. Pick up litter, and leave trees and plants intact.

• **DISPOSE OF HUMAN WASTE PROPERLY** Use toilets whenever possible. If toilets are not available, dig a "cat hole" at least six inches deep and 200 feet from any water, trails, campsites, or the base of climbs. *Always pack out toilet paper.* On big wall routes, use a "poop tube" and carry waste up and off with you (the old "bag toss" is now illegal in many areas).

• **USE EXISTING TRAILS** Cutting switchbacks causes erosion. When walking off-trail, tread lightly, especially in the desert where cryptogamic soils (usually a dark crust) take thousands of years to form and are easily damaged. Be aware that "rim ecologies" (the clifftop) are often highly sensitive to disturbance.

• **BE DISCREET WITH FIXED ANCHORS** *Bolts are controversial and are not a convenience*—don't place 'em unless they are *really* necessary. Camouflage all anchors. Remove unsightly slings from rappel stations (better to use steel chain or welded cold shuts). Bolts sometimes can be used pro-actively to protect fragile resources—consult with your local land manager.

• **RESPECT THE RULES** and speak up when other climbers don't. Expect restrictions in designated wilderness areas, rock art sites, caves, and to protect wildlife, especially nesting birds of prey. *Power drills are illegal in wilderness and all national parks.*

• **PARK AND CAMP IN DESIGNATED AREAS** Some climbing areas require a permit for overnight camping.

• **MAINTAIN A LOW PROFILE** Leave the boom box and day-glo clothing at home—the less climbers are heard and seen, the better.

• **RESPECT PRIVATE PROPERTY** Be courteous to land owners. Don't climb where you're not wanted.

• **JOIN THE ACCESS FUND!** To become a member, make a tax-deductible donation of $25 or more.

The Access Fund

Preserving America's Diverse Climbing Resources
PO Box 17010 Boulder, CO 80308
303.545.6772 • www.accessfund.org

More Climbing Guides from
Falcon® Publishing and Chockstone Press

FALCON®

FALCONGUIDES® Leading the Way™

www.Falcon.com

Since 1979, Falcon® has brought you the best in outdoor recreational guidebooks. Now you can access that same reliable and accurate information online.

❏ <u>Browse our online catalog</u> for the latest Falcon releases on hiking, climbing, biking, scenic driving, and wildlife viewing as well as our Insiders' travel and relocation guides. Our online catalog is updated weekly.

❏ A <u>Tip of the Week</u> from one of our guidebooks or how-to guides. Each Monday we post a new tip that covers anything from how to cross a rushing stream to reading contour lines on a topo map.

❏ A chance to <u>Meet our Staff</u> with photos and short biographies of Falcon staff.

❏ <u>Outdoor forums</u> where you can exchange ideas and tips with other outdoor enthusiasts.

❏ Also <u>Falcon screensavers and panoramic photos</u> of spectacular destinations.

And much more!

Plan your next outdoor adventure at our web site. Point your browser to www.Falcon.com and get FalconGuided!

FALCON®

FALCONGUIDES® Leading the Way™

FALCONGUIDES® are available for where-to-go hiking, mountain biking, rock climbing, walking, scenic driving, fishing, rockhounding, paddling, birding, wildlife viewing, and camping. We also have FalconGuides® on essential outdoor skills and subjects and field identification. The following titles are currently available, but this list grows every year. For a free catalog with a complete list of titles, call FALCON® toll-free at 1-800-582-2665.

BIRDING GUIDES

Birding Georgia
Birding Illinois
Birding Minnesota
Birding Montana
Birding Northern California
Birding Texas
Birding Utah

FIELD GUIDES

Bitterroot: Montana State Flower
Canyon Country Wildflowers
Central Rocky Mountain
  Wildflowers
Chihuahuan Desert Wildflowers
Great Lakes Berry Book
New England Berry Book
Ozark Wildflowers
Pacific Northwest Berry Book
Plants of Arizona
Rare Plants of Colorado
Rocky Mountain Berry Book
Scats & Tracks of the
  Pacific Coast States
Scats & Tracks of the Rocky
  Mountains
Scats & Tracks of the Desert
  Southwest
Sierra Nevada Wildflowers
Southern Rocky Mountain
  Wildflowers
Tallgrass Prairie Wildflowers
Western Trees
Wildflowers of Southwestern Utah

FISHING GUIDES

Fishing Alaska
Fishing the Beartooths
Fishing Florida
Fishing Glacier National Park
Fishing Maine
Fishing Montana
Fishing Wyoming
Fishing Yellowstone Natl. Park
America's Best Bass Fishing
Trout Unlimited's Guide to
  America's 100 Best Trout
  Streams

PADDLING GUIDES

Paddling Minnesota
Paddling Montana
Paddling Okefenoke
Paddling Oregon
Paddling Yellowstone & Grand
  Teton National Parks

ROCKHOUNDING GUIDES

Rockhounding Arizona
Rockhounding California
Rockhounding Colorado
Rockhounding Montana
Rockhounding Nevada
Rockhound's Guide to
  New Mexico
Rockhounding Texas
Rockhounding Utah
Rockhounding Wyoming

HOW-TO GUIDES

Avalanche Aware
Backpacking Tips
Bear Aware
Desert Hiking Tips
Hiking with Dogs
Hiking with Kids
Leave No Trace
Mountain Lion Alert
Reading Weather
Route Finding
Using GPS
Wild Country Companion
Wilderness First Aid
Wilderness Survival

WALKING

Walking Colorado Springs
Walking Denver
Walking Portland
Walking San Francisco
Walking Seattle
Walking St. Louis
Walking Virginia Beach

ROCK CLIMBING GUIDES

Rock Climbing Arizona
Rock Climbing Colorado
Rock Climbing Montana
Rock Climbing New Mexico
  & Texas
Rock Climbing Utah
Rock Climbing Washington

■ *To order any of these books, check with your local bookseller or call FALCON® at 1-800-582-2665.*
www.falcon.com

FALCON®